Marranos

Marranos

The Other of the Other

Donatella Di Cesare

Translated by David Broder

polity

Originally published in Italian as *Marrani: L'altro dell'altro*. © 2018 Giulio Einaudi editore s.p.a., Turin

This English edition © 2020 by Polity Press

Front cover artwork: Rivera, Diego (1886–1957): *French Intervention and the Empire under Maximilian (1862–1867) – The Porfirian Era (1876–1910)*. Left section of 'From the Conquest to 1930', 1929–1935. Mural, West wall. Mexico City, National Palace. © 2020. Photo Schalkwijk/Art Resource/Scala, Florence

Polity Press
65 Bridge Street
Cambridge CB2 1UR, UK

Polity Press
101 Station Landing
Suite 300
Medford, MA 02155, USA

ISBN-13: 978-1-5095-4203-1 (hardback)
ISBN-13: 978-1-5095-4204-8 (paperback)

A catalogue record for this book is available from the British Library.

Library of Congress Cataloging-in-Publication Data
Names: Di Cesare, Donatella, author. | Broder, David, translator.
Title: Marranos : the other of the other / Donatella Di Cesare ; translated by David Broder.
Other titles: Marrani. English
Description: Medford : Polity Press, 2020. | Includes bibliographical references. | Summary: "Why the story of the exile is the heart of the modern condition"-- Provided by publisher.
Identifiers: LCCN 2020012860 (print) | LCCN 2020012861 (ebook) | ISBN 9781509542031 (hardback) | ISBN 9781509542048 (paperback) | ISBN 9781509542055 (epub) | ISBN 9781509543564 (adobe pdf)
Subjects: LCSH: Marranos--History. | Jews--Persecution--Europe--History.
Classification: LCC DS123 .D5313 2020 (print) | LCC DS123 (ebook) | DDC 305.8/92404--dc23
LC record available at https://lccn.loc.gov/2020012860
LC ebook record available at https://lccn.loc.gov/2020012861

Typeset in 11 on 14 Adobe Garamond by
Servis Filmsetting Ltd, Stockport, Cheshire
Printed and bound in Great Britain by CPI Group (UK) Ltd, Croydon

The publisher has used its best endeavours to ensure that the URLs for external websites referred to in this book are correct and active at the time of going to press. However, the publisher has no responsibility for the websites and can make no guarantee that a site will remain live or that the content is or will remain appropriate.

Every effort has been made to trace all copyright holders, but if any have been overlooked the publisher will be pleased to include any necessary credits in any subsequent reprint or edition.

For further information on Polity, visit our website: politybooks.com

Esther had still kept it a secret that she was a Jew. She had not told anyone about her family background.

Book of Esther, 2, 20

Nothing that has ever happened should be regarded as lost for history.

Walter Benjamin[1]

Claims have also been advanced to the effect that the question of marranism was recently closed for good. I don't believe it for a second. There are still sons – and daughters – who, unbeknownst to themselves, incarnate or metempsychosize the ventriloquist specters of their ancestors.

Jacques Derrida, Marx & Sons[2]

1 Walter Benjamin, 'On the Concept of History' in *Illuminations: Essays and Reflections*, New York, Schocken, 1969, p. 253.
2 Jacques Derrida, 'Marx & Sons' in Michael Sprinkler (ed.), *Ghostly Demarcations: A Symposium on Jacques Derrida's* Specters of Marx, London, Verso Books, 1999, p. 262.

Contents

vii

CONTENTS

The Last Jews: To Begin

To speak of marranos, in a historical sense, is to refer to the Jews in Iberia and the Spanish dominions who were forced to convert to Christianity in order to escape exile or death. A result of the political violence and religious intolerance that was symbolized in most extreme form by the Spanish Inquisition, marranism created a lacerated identity, tragically split between two irreconcilable ties of belonging – one external and official and another intimate and hidden. Even once these 'new Christians' had been christened, they remained separate from the 'old Christians', who suspected them of secretly observing the Jewish rites. No *auto da fé* was enough. Suspicions regarding the marranos – who, despite everything, continued to appear unassimilable and extraneous – became so intense that the first racist laws of the modern age were proclaimed, as blood became the criterion for the protection of a supposed purity. The gates of universal brotherhood thus slammed shut.

Persecuted, hunted and tortured, the marranos were pushed back into a cryptic, subterranean existence that compromised their life and undermined its very conditions. They were trapped in a hybrid space, banished into a no-man's-land. There, they kept their inaccessible secret over the centuries, even as they were accused of being infidels, liars and traitors. But this immemorial devotion would have paradoxical results. For the crypto-Judaism, which was conserved at such great pains, ended up holding on to almost nothing of the ancient faith. The marranos stood at a remove from other Jews, with whom their relations weakened or even vanished. They instead elaborated a religion and a way of life that rested on unstable foundations of ambivalence and dissent – as did their identity itself. It was no longer clear to the outside observer whether the marranos were heretical Christians or secret Jews. Nonetheless, a fervent messianic expectation, sustained by the memory of the future, lit up their dark night of exile. Isolated, excluded and segregated, they persisted in their secret, convinced that they were the last Jews on earth.

The marranos long remained clandestine, in the most distant and remote sites of oppression. In some striking cases, they would re-emerge only in the twentieth century. Many others returned to Judaism long before then, whether re-joining old communities or founding new ones. The effect was a disruptive one. For within themselves the marranos bore the seed of doubt, the ferment of opposition. Compelled to be dissidents, they gave rise to radical thinking. Having long lived on the edge, on the border, the marranos were extreme and eccentric – and they fed the emergence of messianic movements that shook institutional religion. Their return marked a profound rupture in tradition, indeed one that could not be healed. From this rupture, Jewish modernity was born.

Having come out into the open, those who considered themselves the last Jews revealed themselves to be the first moderns. The split self, the impossibility of a full belonging, a constitutive extraneousness – this is the marranos' indelible legacy. With them, the myth of identity implodes and shatters.

It is thus necessary to go beyond this term's restrictive historical meaning. In so doing, one can proceed to investigate a phenomenon that has not yet reached its conclusion, just as modernity itself has not been exhausted. This is all the more true given that, in refusing to divulge their secret, the marranos rendered their history invisible, making it impossible to produce a historiography. What, then, remains of the marranos, outside the archive of memory? To reflect on marranism in its complex and articulated sense, retracing its singular paths – without condemnation, but also without apologias – thus means to probe the very foundations of modernity.

Anarchiveable

The marranos' history is not over. To put the final seal on it would, indeed, be a further violence – as if to decree that they had irrevocably disappeared. In recent years, there have been multiple cases of people, sometimes in tragic circumstances, detecting hidden traces of an unknown past. They have guessed, intuited or – thanks to some vague clue – re-awakened the lacerated memories that had been headed towards outright disappearance. These memories were prompted by a letter from a distant relative, a murmured deathbed confession, a photograph discovered by chance, an object appearing in a drawer, the re-evocation of an ancient rituality and of a singular gesture. Above all a name, the family name, which conceals within itself – impenetrable and yet still eloquent – the vicissitudes of entire generations. The marranos of both today and yesterday come back out into the open.

Scattered everywhere, from the south-west of the United States to the north-east of Brazil, from Portugal to Italy, invoking that practice of resistance and memory that has allowed them to survive – over and above any traumatic erasure – they demand not to be condemned to the archives. They ask this out of responsibility towards the secret whose memory they bear. They are, by calling, an-archiveable [*anarchiviabili*]. For they have confronted oblivion and challenged the very basis of

4

arché, the principle of the archive, the order of archiving. Anarchically, they shrink from the remote past of antiquity, as they instead lay claim to a future perfect. And this is the future entrusted to a counter-history of those whom history has forgotten, already almost defeated by the compulsion to find refuge in clandestinity. How, then, can their testimony be recovered? How can they be brought out of the crypt? How can their name be redeemed?

The questions pile up. And, in their own paradoxical way, they reveal the fascinating and enigmatic figure of the marrano, who ingeniously evades any attempt at capture. This has been an irritation to more than one historian. Their inclination is to put an end to the matter by giving a definition of the marrano. They thus force the marrano to declare her identity once and for all and confine her to a closed book. Enough, then, with these marranos! And enough with those who would purport to trespass any further and extend the marranos' presence.

In recent years, however, marranism has left the dominion of official history. Marranos are, indeed, known as navigators of borders. Marranism has come to arouse enormous interest among philosophers, anthropologists, novelists and psychoanalysts. In fact, it was a historian – Jacques Revel – who raised the question of the different modes of being marrano. He both widened its horizontal semantics and marked out its chronological verticality – and, ultimately, its durability. Does there exist a marrano condition? If so, what are its characteristic traits? The marrano ought to be seen, more than as a terminal figure, as an initiating one, who gives rise to a new era of Jewish history and, beyond that, to modernity itself. Yet the modernity to which the marrano gives rise is not a conciliatory and harmonious one, but rather one criss-crossed by an irreparable dissonance. From this flows a long tradition of revolt – one yet to reach its conclusion.

This is why it is possible to detect, within the troubling and spectral figure of the marrano, what Giorgio Agamben has called an 'exemplary paradigm'. Just like the *Homo sacer* or the *Muselmann*, the marrano is both inscribed in history and exceeds its limits. Through her exemplarity she makes it possible to read the phenomena of the present, as she casts light on connections and family ties that may otherwise fall into oblivion.

Romantic Heroes or Cowardly Renegades?

There is perhaps no other figure open to such diverse interpretations. With their singular fate and their unusual double-sided character, the marranos have always brought divided responses, prompting contrasting evaluations. Even their place is not wholly clear. Do they belong to Spanish, or perhaps Portuguese history? Or to Italian or Dutch history? More fundamentally, however, the marranos were the first cosmopolitans. What, then, ought to be said about Jewish history? Should the marranos not be protagonists in this history, at least in part?

In the old ghettos where they spent their existence in study, fear and expectation, the eastern Jews maintained a vague yet hardy memory of the legendary splendour, the prestige and the ostentatiousness of the Sephardim – the Spanish and Portuguese Jews. Does the exploration of the most obscure recesses of the Kabbalah – Jewish mysticism – not, perhaps, owe something to them? And how could one forget the name of Baruch Spinoza? Cultured and audacious, refined and haughty, the marranos were bathed in an aura of enticing exoticism. That was how Rembrandt painted them and that is how Heine immortalized them in his poetry. The fact that some of them may have been Christians for a while did not damage this romantic portrayal. They were *anusim*, forced – that is, they had been subjected to a forced baptism, not to mention the tortures of the Inquisition. They had been tortured, derided, made to suffer. The Spanish disdainfully called them marranos. Precisely for this reason, they deserve to be counted among the long series of Jewish martyrs.

Hidden in clandestinity, the marranos had preserved Judaism in the intimacy of their hearts. They did so even as they outwardly embraced the faith imposed upon them, Christianity. They continued to observe Jewish rites in secret. Their identity held firm, intact and authentic. Once the Christian mask was taken off, they returned to being Jews. For a long time, this romantic, and romanticized, vision was the most widespread one. For evidence of this, one need only leaf through the popular book by Cecil Roth, which right from its first pages speaks of the marranos' 'rare heroism', the 'sheer dramatic appeal' of those Jews who, beyond any mystification, 'remained at heart as they had always been'. It is as if their existence could be divided into two parts, an external and an internal one, without the one having an impact on the other. But those who spread such a consoling idea have no qualms about reiterating an old condemnation – asking why the marranos did not sacrifice themselves. Why, that is, did they not choose to die for *Kiddush Hashem*, the sanctification of the Name, and not follow the noble example of the Jews of the Rhineland, who resolutely faced up to their impending martyrdom?

The answer is often sought in the 'moral difference' between the German and Spanish Jews. It is supposed that, after years of good living, the Spanish Jews had got used to the world around them – and were thus no longer able to react. The Sephardic Jews and the marranos are thus all lumped in together, all equally beaten over the head with an intransigent, moralizing condemnation. This accusation recalls the one implicit in the abject question that was directed at the European Jews after the experience of Nazism: 'why did they go like lambs to the slaughter?'

Apologias and condemnations have followed the marranos around, ending in a paradoxical reaffirmation of their supposedly dual character. Were they courageous or craven, fearless or cowardly, inflexible or prepared to compromise? The romantic saga that was in vogue up to the early twentieth century has gradually given way to more specific studies. The evanescent image of the marranos consigned to a remote past changed – and it did so by way of a sensational discovery. In 1917 Samuel Schwarz – a Polish Jew working as an engineer in Belmonte, in an unpassable and isolated area in northern Portugal – chanced upon flesh-and-blood marranos who still secretly practised Jewish rites. After accepting him with some suspicion and resisting his questions, they ultimately revealed that they were, indeed, *judeos*. Research then multiplied apace. Between 1929 and 1936 Yitzhak Baer gathered and published the documents kept in the archives of the Inquisition. The persecutors themselves had helped to conserve the memory of the marranos. Baer's verdict was clear: the *conversos* – in good measure assimilated, corrupted by rationalist philosophy and made victims of a violent antisemitism – should be considered an integral part of Jewish history.

But what about those marranos who had become

fervent Catholics? Did they not include prominent figures, even rabbis, who had converted in all sincerity and been promoted to the highest ecclesiastical offices? Not to mention Tomás de Torquemada, the Grand Inquisitor. Perhaps these marranos should, then, be inserted into Spanish history. After all, after it erased their presence and denied them citizenship in the pure and integral *patria*, Spain did go back to claiming them as its own. What made Spain unique was not the permanent crusade, but rather the *Convivencia* among Muslims, Jews and Christians. This was the revolutionary thesis advanced in a 1948 book by the powerful anti-Francoite voice Américo Castro. With this, he clearly recognized the importance of the *conversos* who, mostly being heretics, had sowed the seed of dissent.

The enigma of the marranos became denser, rather than clearer; their identity appeared tangled and their belonging controversial. But the Holocaust cast a gloomy shadow over this tormented history, which no longer seemed somehow romantic. Even Roth admitted this in the new edition of his book, which had first been published back in 1931. There were simply too many disturbing similarities between the marranos and the Jews living under Hitler's regime. The marranos could offer a negative example – one not to be followed. For they had, of course, not been devout.

Therefore, the history of the marranos had to be radically reviewed. No, they were not heroes, or martyrs. Rather, they were turncoats and fakers; their lives attested to the threat intrinsic to diaspora, namely the risk of assimilation. Above all, they could not be considered Jews. This was what Benzion Netanyahu asserted in a 1966 book, which triggered a critical revision of this question. His posthumous condemnation was, in fact, founded on the rabbis' own verdicts. Marranism was but a belated and ineffective means of reacting to the Inquisition. This revision sowed the seeds of fresh suspicion. But it also demanded greater caution. Some historians, like Henry Méchoulan, sought to save all that could be saved, by drawing a dividing line between the crypto-Jews, who had remained 'true Jews', and the marranos, who instead chose idolatry by becoming new Christians. But how could one distinguish between them and based on what criteria? How should one evaluate the case of Yitzhak Cardoso, who was not considered a Jew in Madrid but in Verona became one of European Jewry's most prominent representatives?

Yosef H. Yerushalmi in particular opened up new perspectives, as he both inserted the marranos into Jewish history and delimited the boundaries of this phenomenon, the better to interpret its complex pattern. When their verdicts are read properly, it is evident that not even the rabbis were in agreement: some issued reproaches, while others showed indulgence. Certainly, the marranos no longer followed the *halakha*, the Jewish law, and did not observe the many precepts. But was this good reason to disavow them? The rabbis were called on to take practical decisions, regarding the lives and often the survival of those who had remained in captivity, as well as those who had managed to flee. They could only partly shed light on the marranos' condition.

The question remains as to their 'Jewishness' – the term used by Yerushalmi and later adopted by Jacques Derrida. Could the marranos call themselves Jewish? Of what does Jewishness consist? And what, then, does it mean to be Jewish? The definition of the marrano also puts into question the definition of 'Jew'. Peremptory judgements and unilateral definitions that purport to capture the marrano – this fugitive, refugee and renegade – end up masking her ambivalence. They cover up the innate dualism that makes this figure both so fascinating and so troubling.

Esther and Another Sovereignty

The event being recounted is, certainly, not a happy one; for once again, a threat is bearing down on the Jewish people. Yet this is the first time that the word 'annihilation' has appeared. It is pronounced by Haman, the adviser to King Ahasuerus, in the vast Persian Empire. This obscure bureaucrat, the prototype of the exterminator, points to the Jews as enemy number one, insisting that the question will need a final solution. 'And Haman said unto king Ahasuerus, "There is a certain people scattered abroad and dispersed among the people in all the provinces of thy kingdom; and their laws are diverse from all people; neither keep they the king's laws: therefore it is not for the king's profit to suffer them. If it please the king, let it be written that they may be destroyed." '¹ The attribute of the God of Israel – one, *echad* – stigmatized a people subjected to the gravest of political accusations: insubordination, contempt, failure to observe the laws of the realm and perhaps – who knows? – conspiracy. It was neither appropriate nor useful to continue to grant residency to these insubordinate foreigners, who also followed different laws. They were dispersed and hence vulnerable and thus could not put up resistance. And if they had already separated themselves, why not isolate them completely? Cold and methodical, Haman set the machinery of extermination in motion. Their fate was entrusted to the roll of the dice, the drawing of lots – *pur*, hence the name Purim, the festival of lots. And the date was chosen for the annihilation of the Jews, all in a single day: the thirteenth day of the month of Adar. Once the seal was pressed, the edict was handed to couriers so that it could be delivered to the satraps and governors. The apparatus mobilized, in order to prepare the massacre. The order

1 Book of Esther, 3, 8–9. This and all subsequent citations from KJV.

was written as clearly as could be: 'destroy, kill, cause to perish'.[2]

Yet this story has a happy ending. The Jews' fate was turned on its head as they miraculously escaped the massacre. The evil Haman, a dangerous blowhard, instead fell into the trap of his own plot; it was he and his accomplices who ended up on the gallows. This story could rightly be placed in the modern genre of fiction, especially given that it does not concern real events. World history knows nothing of a Jewish queen in the Persian Empire. With its lavish banquets, the court intrigues and its dramatic twists, the famous biblical Book of Esther almost resembles a short story from the *Thousand and One Nights*. It all seems like a fable. Frivolity, irony, caricature and satire follow one after another in a text that does not even mention the Name of God. The Scroll of Esther simulates the Divine self-concealment ('And I will surely hide my face ...', *haster astir*).[3] Yet the Scroll is much more realistic than other biblical tales. Its complexity lies in the multiple inter-sections between both theological and political themes. While the threat that looms over the Jewish people is annihilation, the narrative revolves around the Law, and the final response is messianism.

It all begins with the great banquet provided by

2 Book of Esther, 3, 13.
3 Deuteronomy, 31, 18.

Ahasuerus, who demands that Queen Vashti should be there. He wants to show her to everyone, 'with the royal crown', in order to 'show the people and the princes her beauty'. But Vashti refuses. Perhaps Ahasuerus wanted to show her off to these drunken men, naked. Some commentators suggest this in order to diminish her guilt. Without doubt, this is an unprecedented act of disobedience. The king explodes with rage. Other women could imitate her example and all the husbands in the realm would end up being humiliated just like the king. Vashti bore even greater responsibility because she was meant to be a role model. Her fate is decided: she will no longer appear before the king. Ahasuerus repudiates her, but not before he has brought together his advisers – after all, his affairs are handled in the presence of the wise men who know 'law and judgement'.[4]

The reference to the law, here, may at first look like a strange detail, if not a pointless juridical formality. Yet it also alludes to the relationship between God and Israel. In the figure of Vashti, it is not hard to make out the shape of the Jewish people in exile, which has become distant from the Law, to the point of rebelling against the king. This revolt is especially serious because this is also the people who forever remain an example to others. Exile is not only the framing but also the great theme of the Scroll. The story has its

4 Book of Esther, I, 13.

basis in the condition of the diaspora, whose challenges are described and whose risks are near-prophetically preannounced. But the question mark that torments the Jews is whether the divine edict that set the seal on their exile after the destruction of the Temple is an irrevocable one.

The expression *devar HaMelech* – 'royal edict' – thus recurs repeatedly through this text. In short, will the exile end or not? To adopt again the metaphor of a wedding, is this separation a temporary one, or is this instead a definitive rejection? And if this is a real divorce, is it not then necessary to do away with the marriage contract, the Law, considering it now invalid and thus in need of dissolution? Against the historical backdrop of exile, which puts Jewish existence to the test, what is in question, here, is the Law and respect for the Law. The protagonist of the Scroll is Esther, a messianic figure who intercedes at a point when annihilation already seems inevitable. She is a humble but also powerful symbol of return.

But who is this Esther? What role does she play in a story permeated with worry, punctuated by the word 'deportation' – which sounds some four times – and agitated by the spectre of extermination? How does she save her people, reversing their fate? A foreigner and orphan, she is adopted by Mordecai. An elderly relative and observant Jew, he, however, forbids her from revealing the secret of her birth and the fact that she belongs to the

Jewish people. Although her father was called Avikhail, which means 'my father is value', Esther does not have – cannot have – any kind of arrogance. Rather, she grows up conscious that she is in an extremely weak condition – one caught between melancholia, for the unbridgeable void of an absence that afflicts her from the origin, and a painful reticence, to which she is restricted. Moreover, she lives in a land of exile, where those who worship multiple gods do not look kindly on her faith. Indeed, they are specifically intolerant of monotheism, with its exclusive aspect destined to uproot the pagan divinities. Thus, the Jewish orphan girl gets used to clandestinity. Hadassa – the feminine of *hadas*, referring to the myrtle plant – is the Jewish name her parents gave her. It bears the hope that Hadassa, like the myrtle, will flower all by herself. But she keeps this name for herself, in her own private thoughts. In public she is called Esther, which means 'I will hide myself.' This name reminds her of the imperative of secrecy.

Yet Mordecai is always there by her side. He built up a great deal of credit for himself in the Persian Empire, without ever assimilating or bending to power. Could his inflexibility be the reason for the extermination? Quite the contrary. Precisely because he has remained devoted to his Judaism he is loyal and trustworthy. And the king is well aware of this. If Esther is the symbol of assimilated Judaism, which risks forever distancing itself and prejudicing any chance of return, Mordecai instead represents the Judaism bound to tradition and faithful to the Law. The division between these roles makes the plot of this story even more complex. Esther lives a secret life, in which she is protected by Mordecai and takes recourse to his aid and his advice. What would Esther be without Mordecai? But the inverse is also true. What would Mordecai be without Esther? Like fate itself, in this surprising tale, roles are also continually reversed

After Vashti is spurned, a beauty contest is announced. And Esther wins. This is not the result of myrrh oil, sweet odours and balsams. The Scroll does tell us that Esther is 'fair and beautiful'. But, added to her appeal is that touch of mystery that distinguishes her from all the rest – the interiority of an inerasable secret. When she appears, the king is so struck that he breaks protocol and turns it inside-out. He leads her into the royal residence and has a banquet prepared in her honour. The decisive events play out in the setting of the King's Table. Just as Vashti lost her royal status at a banquet, Esther, in turn, is crowned *malka* – queen – at another one. The figure of Vashti, an Israel that has allowed itself to head into exile, even to the point of repudiating the Law, is replaced by that of Esther, an Israel whom exile has humbled.

But what happens when, thanks to Haman's intrigues, the extermination is decreed? Everyone knows that royal decrees cannot be revoked. So how does Esther pressure

Ahasuerus into cancelling it? When everything seems to have been lost already, Mordecai asks Esther to reveal herself to the king and to 'make request before him for her people'.[5] It is time to come out of clandestinity. And, in turn, Esther orders Mordecai to: 'gather together all the Jews that are present in Shushan, and fast ye for me, and neither eat nor drink for three days, night or day: I also and my maidens will fast likewise and so will I go in unto the king, which is not according to the law: and if I perish, I perish.'[6]

Esther brings down the veil on her secret and attempts the impossible. Her intervention is concentrated in two expressions. The first, which responds to Mordecai's request, is *karov le-malkhut*, 'to go in unto the king'; the second, which describes her own initiative, is *lo ke-dat*, 'not according to the law'. To defend her people accused of lèse majesté, Esther ventures into royal palace – a death sentence to whoever is forbidden entry – and, through her extra-legal action, appealing to a different sovereignty, overturns the lots – the *pur*. The most distant suddenly appears the closest. A Jewish woman assimilated even to the point of no longer declaring herself Jewish, who concealed herself, masked herself, stretches the law to get closer to the king – *karov le-malkhut*. In her *teshuva*, in her return to the king, she manages to get

5 Book of Esther, 4, 8.
6 Book of Esther, 4, 16.

him to go back on his steps, to revoke the irrevocable decree and to cancel the annihilation, reducing it to nil.

Esther secures survival for Mordecai and the whole Jewish people. The salvation comes from her *tikkun*, her withdrawal, into the dark night of exile, which precedes the light of dawn. When she reveals herself, at the last moment, on the very brink of apocalypse, she changes the course of history – defeating Haman, the symbol of evil and of baseless hatred. Esther is a metaphor for the diasporic Jews. She represents a messianism of exile, centred on return. Salvation comes not from a powerful and combative warrior, but rather from a hidden queen to whom the Jewish people's very existence is entrusted. No figure could better illustrate the condition, the history, the fate of the marranos. Precisely because the queen fired their imagination with her audacity, spurred their courage and brought them comfort, the Purim, which seemed to have a connection with the Kippur, the day of expiation, became an extraordinary anniversary, celebrated in the first full moon of February (and not in the month of Adar, as it ought to have been according to the Hebrew calendar).

Through a mystical-poetic reading of the Scroll of Esther they detected the long-awaited turnaround. For the *conversos*, too, the moment of liberation from the power of their enemies would come, eventually. In his *Poem of Queen Esther*, the marrano poet João Pinto Delgado wrote: 'the splendour radiated by her beauty

/ illuminated the night and darkened the day'. Perhaps the sense of the marrano condition lies precisely here – as the day of existence grows darker, life is played out in the negative of the night.

Convert and Flee!

Around 1160, Maimonides' family abandoned Córdoba in order to escape Almohadi's cruel persecutions and crossed the Strait of Gibraltar to make their home in Fez. If the motive for this sudden departure is obvious, the reason for choosing this destination is less clear. Why leave, only to head for the heart of the Empire? Many indicators would suggest a conversion to Islam – a temporary conversion, that is, for the sake of keeping up appearances. The family's journey resumed a few years later, in 1165, as they set course beyond the imperial borders, reaching Alexandria and then al-Fustat, the urban core of Cairo. After a long period of pilgrimages, finally the firstborn Moshe – already known across all the Andalusian communities for his prodigious memory, his rare capacity for concentration, and his immense knowledge, ranging from Talmudic literature to algebra – had an opportunity to demonstrate his gifts. He became doctor to the court of Saladin and established himself not only as the diaspora's most esteemed rabbinical authority, but also as a great philosopher.

Perhaps, however, his thought was too far ahead of its time. His *Guide for the Perplexed*, directed to an enlightened minority, did not so much guide and orient as arouse a perplexity of its own. The bold project of conjugating the Talmud with philosophy thus proved a failure. Nonetheless, the traces left by this errant intellectual, who grasped the delicate questions of his era with near-prophetic farsightedness, were both profound and enduring. The question of forced conversion was already the order of the day and no small number of Jews were passing over to Islam. Perhaps also seeking to defend himself from the accusations levelled against him, Maimonides thus wrote a *Letter on Apostasy*. The authenticity of this letter has sometimes been doubted, precisely because it took on such a thorny theme. But later he also made other interventions on this same topic.

The letter was something close to a manifesto. Here, Maimonides advised against martyrdom, considered not a Jewish norm but rather an exceptional act, a sacrifice that could not be asked of the multitude. He instead indicated a less heroic, more prudent response, holding that if the Jews were threatened with death, they would have no alternative but to opt, temporarily, for dissimulation. Then – continuing to observe as many of the precepts as possible in secret – they should 'abandon all possessions and walk day and night' until they found a place where they could return to their own religion. Not without a certain vehemence, Maimonides also railed against a rabbi who had indiscriminately condemned all the converts. Maimonides' philosophical and auto-biographical reflection addressed the questions raised by the marranos' dramatic history. If whole masses of Jews faced violent conversion, what was to be done? Was there not an alternative to death? Maimonides suggested the possibility that conversion could be interpreted as an internal emigration – one that did not forbid a later return.

When It All Began

Forced conversions were hardly a novelty. Rather, a threshold was crossed – and here the question of the marranos comes into play – in terms of the brutality and the sheer extent of the events now taking place. One can pinpoint a specific date for this (such as rarely takes place in history): 4 June 1391. That day, an incensed crowd burst its way into the *judería* of Seville, headed by the archdeacon Ferrán Martínez – a mouthpiece for the mounting animosity and the ancestral anti-Jewish hatred. Spain was the crossroads of many and diverse peoples and the land of an ever-difficult *Convivencia*. Now, it was gripped by an unstoppable identitarian pas-sion, by a mystical fervour for pure blood. The first victims were the Jews: they were the foreigners, marked by a theological guilt and a social anathema, who undermined identity.

The rabbi and philosopher Hasdai Crescas wrote a short letter recounting the devastation, which was carried out under the motto 'The cross or death!' Few Jews 'sanctified the Name, while many' – he laconically observed – 'violated the Covenant'. There were over four thousand victims. After Seville it was the turn of Córdoba, Toledo, Madrid, Ciudad Real, Burgos, Valencia, Gerona and Barcelona.

Mass killings spread, along with the pillage of whole neighbourhoods and the destruction of synagogues. Some Jewish communities were decimated. Some Jews sought to escape death by being baptized. A first wave of conversions was shortly followed by a second one characterized by a passionate proselytism, a missionary militancy, inspired by the Dominican Vicente Ferrer. How many Jews died and how many converted? It is impossible to know. Baer hypothesized that out of around 600,000 Jews resident in the territories of the crown of Castile, Aragon and Navarra, one-third perished, a third survived and a third saved themselves by way of baptism. These figures are imprecise, exaggerated and doubted by many. Yet they give some symbolic idea of this phenomenon and its reach.

A new figure was thus created: that of the *conversos* or *cristianos nuevos*. And the first effect of forced baptism was division: parents were separated from their children and wives from husbands. According to many accounts, it was, indeed, women who resisted most and for longest. Relegated to the private sphere, marranism managed to stay alive across the centuries in, so to speak, a feminine form, through the quasi-rabbinical authority of the many women who continued the *berakhot* and benedictions, clandestinely celebrating the Jewish holidays.

Between Silence and Nostalgia

The Hebraizing *conversos* were those who, despite their baptism, still felt themselves to be Jews, but were constrained to be Jews only in their own private sphere, as demanded by the temporary evil of dissimulation. They thus suffered a certain coldness – bordering on rejection – shown them by the communities to which they had previously belonged. Indeed, it is hardly surprising that those Jews who had resisted conversion saw the marranos as traitors. After the initial trauma, however, they sought to support them by whatever means they could.

In the public sphere, the Hebraizing converts presented themselves as Christians. They were obliged to recite formulas that they considered idolatrous but, internally, they cancelled out the words coming out of their lips by murmuring ancient benedictions and praying in silence. They persisted in maintaining a form of Jewish life in private. There were still schools and synagogues close by; the fact that they continued to live in the *judería* allowed them to celebrate holidays and observe the Shabbat. It did not take much effort to calculate the dates of the Hebrew calendar, with its complex harmony between the solar and lunar systems; after all, they only had to keep an eye on the fervid preparations going on in the community and cast a sideways glance at the busy goings-on among their neighbours. These latter, in turn, often proved considerate and helpful, to the point of complicity. They brought the marranos hidden books, kosher food, oil for the lamps and all that could help nurture continued links. It is hardly surprising that the records of the Inquisition include an abundance of testimony on the furtive ceremonies and the illegal meetings that were held, from Toledo to Ciudad Real, at least up till 1480, when the first laws were introduced to divide the *conversos* from the Jews. Thus, the marranos, overwhelmed by their sense of guilt and oppressed by the weight of shame, were consigned to their absurd capitivity. Spain was their Egypt. They lived a triple exile – as Jews, they were still in the diaspora, as *conversos* they were excluded from Jewish life, and as Hebraizing Christians they survived in increasingly hostile Catholic surroundings. They did not abandon hope. Yet, over time, it gave way to a bitter nostalgia for an immemorial past.

'New Christians'?

The conversions were not always forced – some Jews voluntarily chose baptism. The most striking case was that of Shlomo Halevi, chief rabbi of Burgos. He had converted even before the devastation of the *judería* and sought to bring the community with him, though only a few did follow. Halevi adopted the symptomatic – and revealing – name Pablo de Santa María. He headed to Paris to study theology and made his career in the ecclesiastical hierarchy, before returning to Burgos as bishop of that city. It goes without saying that, from a Jewish point of view, he was one of the greatest apostates of his time. Indeed, there was uproar over the conviction that had driven him to embrace the cross – namely, his certainty that he was not in fact violating the Covenant, but rather remained within Judaism. For some time already before his conversion, he had been reading the Torah in a Christian key, becoming ever more convinced that, in rejecting Jesus, the Jews had committed a fatal error and precluded their own salvation. It was this that drove him to baptism. This explains why, even when he addressed himself to the Jews, he continued to speak of 'us'.

Surprised and dumbfounded, his close friend Yehoshua Halorki rebuffed Santa María's argument that the Messiah had already arrived. Did peace really everywhere prevail? Did the lamb live together with the wolf? But even these doubts heralded a hesitation, a certain wavering. Some time later, Halorki took part in the famous Disputation of Tortosa under the name Gerónimo de Santa Fe – and the Jews called him *mega-def*, the blasphemer. Rather than bring his friend back to Judaism, Halorki had instead followed him, animated by the same conviction that it was necessary to remain within Judaism but also carry out this further step. And this meant accepting that the Messiah had come already.

Not by accident, the Disputation of Tortosa, which made its solemn opening on 7 February 1413, was entirely centred on messianism. The rabbis found themselves in a difficult position, given both the pressures to which they had been subjected and the need to hold back the oppositionists coming from within the world of Judaism itself. They defended themselves by attempting to distinguish between two messianisms: the Christian one, conceived as redemption from sin and the salvation of the soul, and the Jewish one, instead understood more as a political liberation.

There were a limited number of cases, like that of Shlomo Halevi, who became Pablo de Santa María. But also important was the schema of thought that he introduced. Halevi argued that if, for a pagan, baptism meant accepting a new faith, for a Jew it did not mark a passage to some extraneous doctrine. From where, after all, had Christianity come? Such thinking is also apparent elsewhere, in other direct or indirect accounts. Indeed, within a Christian perspective, the fact that they were Jews ought to constitute an advantage and not an obstacle. This was the *conversos'* manner of reacting to the label of 'new Christians', assigned them by the 'old Christians' in a reiterated theology of substitution. They insisted that, precisely because they were Jews, they were much older than the 'old Christians' themselves. And yet these 'Christian-Jews', who in their own way embodied a marrano dualism, ended up being rejected by both sides. For the Jews they represented a betrayal of the self, while the Christians were embarrassed to be associated with them.

Fate had it that this pattern would play out again also over subsequent eras, right up till the twentieth century, both before the Holocaust and after. The effects were various and highly controversial. Emblematic, in this regard, is the case of the philosopher Franz Rosenzweig. After having long contemplated conversion, he pulled back from the brink of baptism: as he bluntly put it in a 31 October 1913 letter: *Ich bleibe also Jude*, 'So I remain a Jew.' Here he maintained that, precisely because he was a Jew, he was already at the point that a pagan might have reached by way of Christianity.

The Other of the Other

If the marranos' condition was a hybrid one, what were its existential and political consequences? The identitarian passion drove the proud Spanish self, in its search for an authentic integrity, to assimilate and swallow the other within itself – annexing it also at the cost of annihilating it. But this had a paradoxical result, which brought to bear another unforeseen and alarming phenomenon. Previously, the other had been distinct and easily recognizable. Yet, once it had been forcibly introduced into the body of Christianity, it remained other, but now internal to it. Thus, a more subtle and complex alterity began to take form. This was, in part, the revenge of the other over the self – an unexpected repercussion.

The Jew had long been the external and exterior other, stigmatized, excluded and physically ghettoized. This foreigner, whose confines marked a sort of frontline, was a potential enemy. But this was an easily identifiable enemy, against whom more or less bellicose actions – massacres, killings, plundering – could from time to time be perpetrated. Now, the traditional external other gave way to an internal other, as the Jew was replaced by the marrano. All the names that had sprung up to denote this unprecedented figure – the *converso*, the *confeso* or the *cristiano nuevo* – took on a pejorative meaning, in popular idiom as in literary language, indeed on the same footing as marrano, precisely because they alluded to this vague, obscure, elusive new alterity. The forced incorporation could not, therefore, be said to have been completed, or a success.

The marrano was the other within. Though he was forced into an internal emigration, he remained different, inassimilable, inheriting the Jew's alterity. And yet he was no longer a Jew – first of all in the eyes of the Jews. The marrano's new alterity was not, then, merely internal. For with respect to the Jew – the other *par excellence* – the marrano became the other's other. This dual alterity was confirmed and reiterated also in relation to the Christian. Notwithstanding all his efforts to dissimulate and blend in, the marrano was considered a Christian-who-was-not-yet-Christian, which is to say, still a Jew, who had to be kept at a proper distance from the *cristiano viejo*. What sense did violent coercion have, if one alterity was extirpated only in order to introduce another, an elusive and even more redoubtable one? Whether he aspired to remain Jewish or tried to assimilate, the marrano was rejected on both fronts, estranged as the other's other and condemned to a duality with no exit route. Wherever he turned his gaze, his ambivalent and treacherous double image was reflected back at him. This necessarily had repercussions on his own self-perception, for despite himself he ended up believing in this image. This identity, negated at the root, ineluctably split in two, assumed the most diverse forms, which often overlapped and interpenetrated. There were also those who, finding themselves caught in this bind, left both religions behind and found an exit route in secular atheism. But from the *conversos* who secretly remained Jews to zealous Catholics, from dissidents to conformists, from heretics to deists, the marranos were confined to a divided, split self, a self in which the other preserved within was a constituent part.

Not only the doubtful and hesitating marranos ended up ensnared in this dual self. So, too, did those who had made a decisive and unambiguous choice. Notwithstanding their every effort, their attitudes, words and gestures betrayed the other, which they imagined they had forever banished. Even the most Hebraizing *converso* did not manage to be entirely Jewish; even from the most fervent Catholic there transpired some small residue of Jewishness. Extraneousness, dissidence, the impossibility of being one's own self – such were the distinctive traits of the marrano, who, through her very existence, heralded the modern condition. For her obligatory doubleness was the mirror that shattered the no less fragmented and divided identity of others.

An Existential Duplicity

Whoever finds herself caught between two different traditions can try to reconcile them, perhaps arriving at some original harmony between them. Ever since antiquity (and up to the present), there have been recurring phenomena of syncretism, notably in the field of religion. And yet the three monotheisms are incompatible rivals. One may quite legitimately recognize similarities and themes where there is a certain convergence; but it is not possible to follow two different paths at once. The incompatibility was accentuated yet further in the time of forced conversions, as one religion sought to erase the other. The tension that shook each *converso* was profound and irreparable. Baptism proved to be an insuperable metaphysical barrier. For, in banishing her into a no-man's-land – in between Jewishness and Christianity, into the space where each excluded the other – it condemned her to duality. It doomed her to the laceration of an internal split, even before any torture. One can imagine the efforts that were made to continue a Jewish form of life in secret, maintaining a distinction between gestures, actions and words. But how could one avoid confusion – or betraying oneself? Pretending to be someone else became a necessity.

Dissimulation is the characteristic trait of the marrano's existence, the one that both concentrates her ambivalent protest and contains her veiled dissent. But it is important to avoid misunderstandings here. The duplicity does not play out as a contrast between one sphere considered reality and another considered as a matter of appearances, as if separated by a sharp dividing line. If that were the case, then the marrano would have kept intact the reality of her Jewishness, even behind the semblance of Christianity. But things were not as simple as that. Vigilant and on the alert in order to protect that dividing line and escape suspicion, the marrano ended up no longer distinguishing between them. For the appearance of things instead turned into reality and reality into appearance. If it is repeated, a simulated gesture becomes a natural habit; if it perennially goes unsatisfied, a sincere aspiration becomes fiction and disappears. Public life penetrates into private life; private life must cautiously make itself public. The boundaries between them explode. They will inevitably become mixed up and confused.

Marranism is duplicity in an extra-moral sense, a duality that marks existence, impairs and divides it. The marrano is compelled to move incessantly between one pole and another, going back and forth without respite. She no longer has a centre. And what she believed to be an identity instead breaks up into a kaleidoscope of reflection and speculation. The ellipse, with its two focal points, could be the image that best responds to this movement. Marranism is the distress born of duplicity. The marrano cannot free herself of the paradoxical ambivalence within which she is caught, of the duality that cuts through her relationship with others but also with herself. Constantly monitored, she learns also to monitor herself, in order to monitor others. Under surveillance, she in turn surveys, from the edge of a paranoid hyperawareness, the result of an ineluctable mania for persecution. Her gaze becomes duplicate, as she strives to assume the point of view of others in order to scrutinize the projection of her own self, in the attempt to examine her own image as reflected by the other. This is a gaze that watches itself, one on the brink of schizophrenia. The marrano watches herself play a role: the role that is assigned her in public space. Driven to lie, to pretend, she learns to feel the hypocrisy in advance, to sniff the trick coming, to resolve the contradictions, to learn to sense the truth in the lies of others.

The marrano is a cryptomaniac by necessity. She encrypts and decrypts without pause. Subtlety, shrewdness and presence of mind are the talents she must cultivate. This, not only in order to cover her intentions, but to unmask others'. Each face is a mask. If every Jew has had to become a Christian, then behind each Christian there is a Jew hiding. And what goes for the self goes also for the other. Forced to betray two faiths, to trick confidence itself, she is condemned to an inexhaustible diffidence. She cannot even trust herself. She lives in constant fear of betraying herself. What trait, what behaviour, what syllable will expose her? This is the fear of the other and also the fear of the self: for the self is a stranger, a sort of clandestine, seditious rival who has to be kept under control and hidden away.

But this double gaze is a privileged vision.

Dissimulation opens onto introspection. What Baltasar Gracián called *mirar por dentro* is not only a path into the soul. One looks within oneself in order to verify that nothing can be intercepted by the other, to be assured of not being caught by surprise. Knowledge of one's own self is the path to better hiding oneself from the eyes of others. Hence why this introspection is political in character – as clearly emerges in the works of Montaigne, who was himself a marrano. It is vigilant because it has its origins in suspicion and descends from surveillance.

The Discovery of the Self

The marrano is not, therefore, just a secret Jew. She is the other's other. She is doubly alienated, persecuted by Christians because she is Jewish and spurned by Jews because she is Christian. This double non-belonging – no matter how painful and lacerating – submits her to an unprecedented existential duplicity, reflected also in the way that she perceives and looks at herself. The marrano watches herself, in her bid to appear similar to a Christian, or, indeed, as she Hebraizes and behaves as a Jew, operating on the tenuous thread of memory. As she swings between the two focuses of the ellipse, passing inexorably from the one to the other, she scrutinizes an inner self, which she had previously ignored and neglected, as she now explores its complex depths.

This is a many-faced self – one that has become elusive, in the bid to escape suspicion. It no longer allows identification. Fragmented, disunited, its identity can at most be recomposed, in ever-new forms, in the pattern of a narration, an autobiographical exertion to alleviate the anguish of duplicity and keep at bay the looming schizophrenia. If external emigration leads to the discovery of the New World, internal emigration leads to the discovery of the self. Both are the outcome of the marrano adventure: yet the latter is no less disruptive than the first.

What drives the marrano towards interiority is her own resistance, dissent, opposition. For whoever is excluded, banished, ever more isolated, lacking a community, the inner self assumes an importance that was previously unthinkable. It is the safe that holds the secret, the site of refuge, the home of an incessant dialogue with a self that one knows, scrutinizes and surveils. But there are multiple paths criss-crossing this new-found land of intimacy. They vary from ascetic mysticism to rationalist philosophy, from Teresa of Ávila to Spinoza.

In the past, the individual inserted within some tradition would acquire ideas and customs from it, to the point of complete identification; from this sprang the illusion of an integral identity. When this bond breaks and reintegration appears artificial, the self becomes the internal tribunal, destined to enjoy an authority greater than any convention. It becomes the space of consciousness. Thus emerges the modernity to which marranism is the prelude. However, the modern self – the autonomous subject described by Hegel – can presume to overcome the internal split. It can purport, through its triumphal march, to elevate itself to the universalism of reason. Conversely, the inner self discovered by the marranos remains divided, for there is no possibility that the wound of the split will heal.

Water and Blood: From Toledo to Nuremberg

Some rushed to the baptismal font spontaneously, while others had to be violently dragged there. Most subjected themselves to this rite as a pre-emptive move, in order to ward off any danger. Indeed, the ecclesiastical canon disapproved of forced baptisms. But what did 'force' really mean? If the victims did not protest out loud, but rather consented for the sake of 'their own salvation', there would be no proofs of coercion and the sacrament had to be considered valid. Dozens, hundreds, sometimes even thousands, of people were baptized en masse. They almost ran out of water. Though it is difficult to hypothesize precise figures, when dealing with the history of the marranos, it is calculated that in the quarter-century between 1391 and

1415 the Jewish communities lost over a hundred thousand members.

The passage from one religion to another was meant to banish any attempt at discrimination. Following its universal vocation, the Church ought to have welcomed the new converts, in a spirit of brotherhood. But that was not how things went. Soon enough, the zeal of proselytism, which could boast spectacular results, gave way to an irrepressible suspicion. Ought these neophytes and their sincerity not, perhaps, be distrusted? Had they not introduced the seed of heresy? The Spanish Jews embodied the contradiction in which the Church was trapped, the paradox that risked frustrating any effort at evangelism.

Nonetheless, it was among the people that the suspicion took root – and came to have deadly effects. The old Jews had changed their names, abandoned some of their habits and changed a couple of their ways of acting. But Jews they remained. One should not, then, be tricked. Behind every Christian there hid a marrano and behind every marrano a Jew. The conversions themselves brought matters to a head: if previously the Jew had been easily recognizable, the trappings of Christianity instead camouflaged her, thus making her far more insidious. The enemy had become invisible. The foreigner had concealed herself in a murky and treacherous unfamiliarity. These hurriedly baptized Jews, artificially introduced into the political body of

Christianity, seemed not to fit into any known category. They had something hybrid and deceitful about them, simply because they jeopardized the centuries-old boundaries. If they were no longer Jews, they were certainly not Christians.

What to call them? The term *conversos* was too neutral and suggested that their conversion had indeed been realized. The preference was to speak of *cristianos nuevos* in order to distinguish them from *cristianos viejos* – in short, from those who were really Christians and had always been so from their origins, rather than pretend ones. The new Christians' arrival in public life sparked feelings of resentment, jealousy and rancour. From the state apparatus to the financial administration, from the corporations to the guilds (including the universities) and religious orders. The doors of fields that had long been off limits to them were flung open. Scattered everywhere, through their endeavours the marranos managed to make headway, sealing matrimonial alliances with the nobility and consolidating their ties with the royal court.

How could this unexpected intrusion be resisted? The hostility built up day after day, intensified by economic hardships and the identitarian passion. In the eyes of the old Christians, the Jews had insinuated themselves under false pretences: these marranos had sneakily taken advantage of baptism in order to get around the legal obstacles and the restrictions of the past. New laws thus needed to be devised. This was itself a bit of nonsense: after so much zeal in removing the barriers of faith, there was now a bid to set up new ones. But if one could no longer look to religion as the dividing line, what other criterion was there for the special legislation against the *conversos*, now being demanded?

Finding any straightforward difference outside religious faith was no simple matter. There was, nonetheless, an obstinate search for it. It was imagined that the distinctive criterion was to be identified in the blood. The old Christians had a pure and untarnished blood, whereas the new Christians had impure, Jewish blood. And water counted for nothing against blood. Not even the holy water of the baptismal font could ever have cleaned off the wickedness of the Jews; no conversion could be the remedy for that 'incurable evil'. The Jewish essence was identified in blood, that fluid so vital and corporeal, secret and ineffable. The *conversos* were thus 'polluted' and barriers were needed in order to avoid contagion. Blood purity became much more important than purity of faith. The criterion for being a true Spaniard was *limpieza de sangre*.

The 'Jewish question' emerged in the era of the marranos If the water still promised salvation, the blood allowed no escape. An insurmountable barrier was erected. This was no longer a matter of Judaism but of Jewish descent. Despite his baptism, a *converso* maintained the proverbial Jewish traits – from cunning to greed, from rigidness to obstinacy – which thus became indelible and inalterable. Even though these are moral and cultural characterizations, they were in fact transmitted by the blood – something impossible to change. This was the unprecedented idea of immutability. The blood was both its bodily vehicle and psychic symbol, in a dangerous and continual oscillation. The soul itself – the theologist Juan Escobar del Corro ruled – was ultimately conditioned by it. Hence why there was no remedy to *converso* blood.

But what was then to be said of Jesus of Nazareth, who himself came from an indelibly Jewish lineage? What answer could there be to such a question troubling Christianity from within? Nazi theology would ultimately concoct an 'Aryan Christ'.

But in the Spain of the *Reconquista*, enflamed by the myth of purity, the doctrine of the physical–moral gap between Jews and Christians was already taking form. Added to the need for self-defence from Jewish blood, imbued with wickedness, was that of keeping the Eucharistic blood intact. As well as representing an element of Christian initiation much more powerful than the baptismal water, this was also the fluid that united the faithful in the mystical body of the Church, understood as a community of blood. The old Christian anti-Judaism merged with a new and modern antisemitism, which furiously intensified some of its theological themes, of which it provided an eminently political reading.

This conjuncture explains the nexus – even if an indirect one – that Yerushalmi recognizes between the Iberian and German models. Both cases headed through the same phases: the semblance of assimilation, a resentment that explodes from below, and legalized discrimination. The birth certificate for the first racist theory reads Toledo, 5 June 1449. This date saw the promulgation of the *Sentencia-Estatuto*, the document on blood purity, which harboured all future 'racial laws'. The text demanded, among other things, that *conversos* of Jewish origin should be barred access to municipal or ecclesiastic posts, and whatever office they could use to harm 'pure origin' Christians. Together with the concept of purity, identified with blood and lineage, the need was also asserted for defence against any possible contagion. *Schutz* – protection – is also the term that recurs throughout the laws issued by the Third Reich in 1935. There was but a short step from Toledo to Nuremberg. Yet, at first, Spain reacted against this, with the spread of political resistance and theological objections. There was a chorus of protests against the law – and it was suspended. As well as a scandal for Christianity, a religion that professed universal brotherhood, the law was also a danger without measure in a country where the blood of Jews, Moors and Christians had mixed for centuries. Yet, though it encountered strong opposition, *limpieza de sangre* did ineluctably assert itself and the statutes did ultimately spread. This demand, which the lower clergy and the common people had never ceased to push, was forcefully reiterated and in 1555 it secured the king's formal approval as well as papal ratification. In 1580 Portugal, too, accepted the statutes. *Limpieza de sangre* became a formal requirement for entering into public life. And this was also a continual vexation, because it was everywhere necessary to show one's *pruebas* – the proofs of purity. And not everyone, even among the old Christians, was exactly immaculate. For instance, the nobility, who had built close family ties with the new Christians, had already been contaminated for some time. It was certainly better to be a son of a nobody and be able to boast of pure origins, like Sancho Panza – 'well-born and at least an old Christian' – than to be a half-Jewish *hidalgo*. Blood purity, as opposed to nobility, became the principle of identity for the mass of the people and the instrument of their vengeance. Origin no longer referred to noble lineage, but rather indicated a line of descent uncontaminated by any strange blood. Though few Spaniards could boast of being 'well-born', *cristianos viejos lindos*, an obsession began for genealogy, accompanied by a repugnant arithmetic of race, which counted each quarter, seventh or tenth of impure blood.

The Great Purge

The expulsion order marked one of the great fractures in Jewish history, an unexpected cataclysm. This was the final loss of Sepharad, the Spanish Jerusalem. The concentration of so many decisive events in one same year – 1492 – was certainly no accident. In January the Catholic Monarchs' victorious armies entered Granada, sealing the end of the *Reconquista*. On 3 August the ships of Christopher Columbus set out from Palos de la Frontera towards the New World. A few days earlier, on 31 July, the last Jew had left Spain.

Promulgated on 31 March 1492, the edict also decreed the end of a large proportion of Italian Judaism, first in Sicily then in Sardinia and the rest of the South – Naples included. This had devastating effects. Then came a third wave of conversions, whose extent is impossible to calculate. It would be more accurate to speak of a purge. The Jews were, indeed, expelled also in order to solve once and for all the problem of the marranos, who put up resistance and seemed stubbornly inassimilable. Even the Tribunal of the Inquisition, established in 1478, did not produce the hoped-for outcomes. The *conversos* did not really want to convert and their souls risked not being saved. Expelling the Jews, the traditionally extraneous other, ought to have allowed the swallowing up of the marranos, the internal other. Separated from the Jewish communities – the ancient *aljamas* who had supported them, notwithstanding any conflictual relations – the marranos in Spain remained segregated.

It seems that at least a third of the Spanish Jews, who had taken to the sea, were ultimately swallowed up by the tides. Safer was passage to Portugal, where they were welcomed as refugees. But this refuge itself proved to be a trap. In 1497, mass conversion was imposed upon them, instead of expulsion. The 'standing baptisms', carried out in a hurry in order to prevent flight, were a singular phenomenon of religicide. The fourth wave of conversions explains the peculiar characteristics of Portuguese marranism, which, notwithstanding fierce cases of persecution and the great massacre of Lisbon in 1506, endured for an extraordinarily long time and would subsequently expand on a vast scale.

Flight and Withdrawal

A double betrayal, a double exclusion. Extraneous to any sense of belonging, the marranos were not, however, expelled. On the contrary, they were kept there by force, waiting to be more or less brutally assimilated and incorporated within the body of the new *state-in-becoming*. They were, at once, included and excluded. A new form of discrimination was taking shape, responding to their unprecedented alterity. If the expulsion edict condemned the Jews to wander far and wide, the marra-nos were stopped from going anywhere else. They were instead condemned to a place where all hospitality was denied them. It was here that the ferocious prosecutors sought to deal with them, to arrest them in order to suss out their secret. Thus, in order to evade capture, the marranos decided on flight.

Remembering the lesson of Maimonides and the route indicated by philosophy, they preferred to save their lives rather than sacrifice them. This, even at the price of taking refuge in a temporary, or seeming, apos-tasy. No blood was to be spilt. There was no pretence of sanctifying the loss of life. The onrush of violence was interrupted. The flight of the marranos was, first of all, this interruption. This move ought not be underesti-mated. It was a gesture that – if often misunderstood, misinterpreted and deplored in moralistic terms – harboured the seed of modernity. This was not only horror faced with the atrocity of torture; indeed, many marranos were subjected to heinous agonies. Rather, the aura of the martyr diminished and the myth of martyrdom fragmented. And doubt crept in as to what truth death could really attest to. With the deceit – the false confession that preserved the marranos' life – this centuries-long, totalizing bind between truth and death fragmented. In this sense, marranism is the opposite of every fundamentalism.

Pursued by the Inquisitors and their merciless will to

examine, identify and assimilate, the marranos fled suspicion and kept their secret safe. They were assailed by worries, and apprehension and anxiety marked their very existence. When they could, they set course for other shores, freeing themselves from the chains of their captivity. However, this happened much later, when links were already broken and bonds and alliances violated. What, then, can flight mean, in the absence of space and exit routes? The marranos beat the paths of discretion, dissimulation and concealment. Unsurprisingly they were accused of evasiveness, deceit and conspiracy. But their evasiveness was first of all coerced. Repeated without relent, it was not an attempt to lead others astray, but rather a long and winding path to evade the grip of others.

If flight cannot mean wandering – unfolding across the horizontal space – it surely means the bid for survival made by those who go around and around in search of a hidden exit route. It is not an exodus, but rather a withdrawal. There is no crossing or still less an advance. For the marranos, flight was a withdrawal – an exile within exile. In an inhospitable terrain where they had no space into which to flee, it was no longer enough to adopt a disguise, to cross one threshold of self-betrayal after another. They obscured themselves, found refuge in non-appearance and journeyed into the cryptic. Crypto-Jews, they segregated themselves in the name of their secret. They lost their right to the light of day. Such was the long night of the marranos.

Yet the crypt is not only a refuge. Their clandestine endurance was a resistance. Moreover, as Dostoyevsky teaches us, the revolt is prepared in the subsoil. All subversion is, first of all, underground. Refugees in the crypt, in the recesses of its depth, the marranos bring to mind those Jews, often mixed with Christians, condemned to exist in the catacombs under the ground in ancient Rome.

The Theology of the Marranos

Even once the marranos had become separated from the other Jews, at first it was not difficult for them to preserve Jewish rites, ceremonies and habits. Subsequently they became dependent on the faithfulness of their memories. Yet, whatever their tenacity, obstinacy and commitment, their memory could not help but fade and their knowledge decline. Segregated from the rest of the Jewish world, they unlearned its language, forgot its liturgy, overlooked its precepts and neglected its customs. With public, active observance impossible, the Jewish way of life gave way to an intimate religiosity characterized by secrecy – one that was confined to the private and interior sphere. The eclipse of a shared tradition, which ought to have assured a unifying bond, ended up bringing about not only the inevitable individual dissimulation but also a variety of forms of worship.

Hollowed out and fragmented, the religion of the marranos took on different hues and realized itself in the plural.

It is, nonetheless, possible to make out family resemblances and to identify the characteristic traits of a peculiar theology. In its constitutive dualism, this theology was both Christian in some elements and Jewish by aspiration. Its fundamental creed was concise and easy to memorize: it held that salvation lay only in Moses' law and that the Messiah was yet to come. Repeated hundreds of times, from the torture chambers to prayers, to chants, the initiations of children and the burning stakes of the *autos da fé*, these two articles encapsulated the unshaken core of marrano theology. Over time they had come to substitute for the confession of Jewish faith, the *Shema Yisrael*, 'listen, Israel'. Indeed, what Jew would have been preoccupied about his own individual salvation? Or the soul separated from the body? And which of them would have imagined he could guarantee it for himself only through his own religion? Nonetheless, one can detect that the 'salvation of the soul' – such a deeply Catholic concern – was not a formula suggested by the jargon of the Inquisitors but rather one that responded to the affliction of the marrano herself. She knew that in this life she was breaking the Jewish law. But she looked, Christian-like, to an afterlife where her soul could, perhaps, be redeemed.

Even at its core, this theology was double – split.

Internally, the marrano repeated Jewish contents and intentions up till death, without ever giving up. But precisely through her opposition, she ended up confirming, despite herself, the significance of the Catholic conceptual context against which she rebelled. Her dissonance was not, therefore, the contingent outcome of an unsuccessful syncretism: rather, it revealed a profound duality.

God is one – there could be no triune Godhead. The marranos came out into the world and they took the message of Judaism with them. They never accepted the doctrine of the Trinity nor that of the incarnation, which were each considered idolatrous. They also considered the images that they contemplated in the churches to be idolatrous, though they sometimes held them in a certain admiration. They were not only influenced by the Jewish ban on images – something that they had not forgotten. Forced to simulate and to respect the appearance and forms of Catholicism, they moreover detested its theatrical character, its performance, the triumph of images. They retreated into their secret intimacy where they remained faithful to the invisible God. To highlight this fundamental difference, they introduced into Spanish the singular *el Dio*, instead of the normal *Dios*, which sounded plural; removing the final 's' showed their dissent and emphasized the singular and unique. In Latin they stopped at the *Gloria patri*. 'In the name of the Lord, Adonai, amen' was their preferred clause.

If they had retreated into themselves, secluded in their secret faith, how did they practise their religion? What about their everyday rites and holidays, in a Judaism that had been conserved only in part – not least when it was ever more atrophied, inadvertently changed, mixed in with Christian themes and customs and, above all, impoverished by risk and fear, maimed and filled with holes on account of the lack of sources? The thinning of a doctrine almost exclusively reliant on oral transmission, the forgetting of customs, and the increasing uncertainty on how to behave, had the effect that the marrano religion differed from Judaism not only in terms of what it added on. Whenever in doubt, it was better to abstain. Bans and prohibitions would usually prevail.

What compensated for the void was renunciation. It was important to prevent any apostasy. But the inner refusal of the Catholic form ended up having repercussions on the Jewish contents themselves. This negation then transformed into a sort of privation, not without the prior influence of the Catholic concept of sacrifice. Thus the marranos' religion was a Judaism by subtraction. The amount of fasting multiplied, while it became almost impossible to celebrate joyous holidays. Besides an atmosphere of profound mournfulness, it was thus dominated by loss and discomfort. The marranos were well aware that their Judaism was incomplete. Yet the failure to observe the precepts induced an acute sense of impotence, a demoralizing frustration. Nothing could mitigate the distress produced by this paradoxical condition: no matter what efforts she made, the crypto-Jew did not succeed in really being a Jew. She was in danger because she was guilty. In the constitutive dualism of the marrano, sin and guilt doubled. For added in was a discomfort regarding the new faith to which she had, in appearance, adhered. This double weight oppressed the very existence of the marrano, who had chosen an inner emigration. Whether this was a Jewish concept of guilt, an original sin of Catholic stamp, or an amalgam of both, the only seeming remedy was expiation.

The greater the danger of being discovered became, the more Judaism was changed and hollowed out. With the passing of the years, the last residues of liturgy also faded. Ultimately, all that still made itself heard was Adonai, barely whispered. In the clandestine period the marranos could lay their hands on various sources. Given that the Talmud was inaccessible and the Jewish texts (including even translations) were confiscated, they concentrated on the Old Testament, maintained by the Church in its biblical canon, and they tried to take it to the letter, interpreting it in the context of their own tragic situation. They attributed particular importance to the psalms and the texts of the prophets. There were scholars and rabbis who, defying the risks involved, set out from Thessaloniki, Venice, Marseilles and other Jewish communities to make their way into the Iberian Peninsula, bringing not only the *siddurim* – the books of prayer – but also their own knowledge. As paradoxical as it may seem, the edicts published by the Inquisition were decisive in this sense, precisely because they gathered together the proofs against the 'heretics' and the 'Hebraizing' condemned to *autos da fé*. Beliefs, practices, customs were conserved thanks to the Holy Office's own punctilious zeal. Such was the case of the recipe for *adafina* (the Sephardic version of *cholent* or *hamin*), a complex and delicious dish prepared for the Shabbat. Thus, against its own intentions the Inquisition became a sort of school of Judaism. But given that the information was often inaccurate, the Inquisitors ended up also being innovators, contributing to the development of a peculiar religion.

When did a new Christian discover himself to be a crypto-Jew? When was he initiated in the secret of the marranos, so carefully and circumspectly preserved in the intimacy of the family? It was not easy to find a solution to such a dilemma. If the children raised as devout Catholics had learned the secret too early they could have inadvertently revealed it, jeopardizing the lives of all concerned. Yet, if there was too long a wait, Catholicism would have had its way already. Many accounts report that the *bar mitzvah* was thus chosen for this purpose – that is, the date at the end of the thirteenth year that, according to Jewish rite, marks the passage into adulthood. In the case of the new

Christians, however, this meant the passage into clandestinity, an initiation in the mysteries and the forms of worship proper to marranism.

This was also the moment at which the Jewish name furtively attributed upon the baptism ceremony was ultimately revealed to the children themselves. The initiation was, necessarily, a traumatic event. The children discovered that they were not what they thought they were or were meant to have been: simply good Christians. On the contrary, they were Christians only in appearance, or rather hidden Jews, and not even really Jews. Their identity was split, segmented and fragmented. The laceration had repercussions on the past and cast a shadow over the future. Unless they, in turn, wanted to betray it, they would be forced to share the secret and forever live in this secrecy. Inadequacy mixed with guilt, a pungent sense of rebellion with the request for pardon.

Unsurprisingly, as many rites disappeared – starting with circumcision – as many practices were forgotten and as more than one festival, like Rosh Hashanah, the Hebrew New Year, fell into disuse, a special significance was attributed to the Kippur. Interpreting the Hebrew term only by assonance, the marranos called it *el día puro*, the pure day, or day of purification. But it was also known as *ayuno mayor*, the great fast. *Quipur, antepur, equipur, cinquepur* – even if it was distorted, the term was preserved for centuries and was one of the most enduring that remains. The marranos strove as best they could to celebrate that solemn day of expiation by fasting, lighting candles 'for the living and the dead', reciting psalms and contemplating the messianic prophesies from the Bible. They asked each other for forgiveness for the insults made and received, in accordance with the traditional Hebrew praxis. But how could they beg pardon for the sin that marked their existence from the very origin, an original sin from which they would never be freed? How could they confess the truth, if the deceit had to be repeated? How could they promise not to fall into sin, if they lived in transgression, if their life was a perennial fall? This marrano duality, which consumed and prejudiced their very being, would not vanish even after Yom Kippur.

In the hour before sunset, the old and dramatic melody of the *Kol Nidre* rang out. The vows were cancelled and the proscriptions taken away. But for the marranos, this ceremony must have represented the height of torment. At the moment at which they ought to have been readmitted into the community, they were instead forced to exclude themselves, asking in advance for the erasure of their deeds over the year to come.

They consoled themselves by recalling that in Judaism sin is not inerasable. Were the great protagonists of the biblical stories not themselves marked by guilt? Why, then, did the poor marranos have to lose hope? Had King David, from whom the Messiah's dynasty emerged, not himself been pardoned? Indeed, counter to the Christian messiah born from virginal purity, the Jewish messiah came from a bastard line. They looked favourably on the figure of Ruth, the Moabite who had bound herself to the Jewish people: in their eyes she showed that the barriers were not insuperable and that one day a reunion would be possible. But, above all, they identified with the Queen Esther who, hiding her own religion – and thus compelled to violate Jewish law – had saved her people from extermination. They detected, in the history of this *avant la lettre* marrano, the premonition of their own fate. A sister, a mother, a 'patron saint' – a wholly Catholic concept – the queen was sanctified and became *Rhaina Santa Ester*, using a Portuguese turn of phrase that was long maintained. Precisely because this bold queen so fired their imaginations, spurred their courage and brought them comfort, the Purim, which seemed to have a connection with the Kippur, the day of expiation, became an extraordinary anniversary, celebrated in the first full moon of February (and not in the month of Adar, as it ought to have been according to the Hebrew calendar). Yet for the marranos it was not a holiday: they had no salvation or, still less, a victory to celebrate. It would have made no sense to give themselves over to drunkenness or the joyful game of masks – for they were forced to mask themselves every day. As they awaited a shrouded miracle, the fast of Esther, which ought to have been observed on the eve of Yom Kippur, was prolonged for three days, just as the biblical tale stipulated.

Even as the season of holidays was stripped to its bones, Pesach – Passover, recalling the liberation out of Egypt – retained a decisive importance. Though they no longer had available the Haggadah, the text read during the ritual Passover Seder dinner, the marranos celebrated Pesach with particular fervour, taking the biblical precept to the letter. Thus – following a custom that the Jews had long abandoned – they consumed the lamb whole, cane in hand, ready to leave their Egypt at any moment. Added to this invention was a further one: the baking of unleavened bread, called 'Holy Bread', out of association with the Eucharist. During its preparation, part of the dough was burned and a vague recollection of the Jewish religious practice followed with the *challah*, the Sabbath bread. (In the rest of the text Sabbath is referred to as Shabbat. The first is in English, the second is a transliteration of the Hebrew name.) Over time, the baking of unleavened bread – a practice that attracted the Inquisitors' watchful eye – became a ceremony no less important than the Seder.

They tried to change the dates to evade checks, subjected the memory to an exhausting pressure and, when this no longer sustained them, they invented new rites to replace the ones that would have betrayed them. In so doing, they drew inspiration from Bible verses or from whatever of the ancient texts they could still recall.

They composed prayers in verses, of which only a few dozen pages still remain. Reliant on oral tradition, the liturgy was reduced and simplified: Hebrew gave way to Judeo-Spanish, Castilian, Portuguese and Latin. Many Catholic themes were adopted in their rituals. They kneeled rather than remain standing. Though they shunned martyrdom, they honoured their martyrs who had been tortured and burned at the stake, or rather venerated them, to the point of making them almost Christian saints to be prayed for. They abandoned all overt Jewish signs: the *Tefillin* (phylacteries), the *Kippah* (yarmulke), the *Talit* (tallit). But they continued to face East.

The memory of the Shabbat, considered the fulcrum of Jewish life, never disappeared. But to celebrate it was a risk. How, indeed, could they abstain from work? They thus resorted to a kind of expedient, though they did not manage to observe a public practice, which would have exposed them to the danger of being easily recognized. The Shabbat was confined to the private sphere and it was thus deprived of its political value. Here, too, renunciation, sacrifice and removal prevailed. They no longer managed to follow the Kashrut rules governing food and were forced to eat forbidden foods in order to evade suspicion. But the Shabbat instead became a fast day, on which they abstained from eating meat. Their reaction was a Catholic one – indeed, something unthinkable in Judaism. For the marranos of Belmonte, it was a surprise to discover that the Jews ate meat on the Shabbat. Moreover, the dualism in which they lived drove them into peculiar forms of compromise and combination. The marranos' religion was made up of small islands of purity amid a sea of transgression.

The marranos continued to light the candles on Friday night in order to celebrate the beginning of the Shabbat. They perhaps did so in a remote corner of the house, in a cellar or attic, hidden within a vase, sheltered from inquiring eyes, this light – a bind that could also compromise them – did not go out even in the darkest times of persecution. This fidelity explains the perpetuation of a secondary anniversary like Hanukkah, which survived under the name 'the festival of candles'. Unbound even from the Shabbat, for the marranos the lighting of the candles became a rite unto itself. When all memory had already been lost, they continued, clandestinely, to light a candle – often no longer even knowing why. It was the unconfessed symbol of marranism.

Upon deaths, the marranos also maintained the Jewish rites or, at least, tried to do so. After the unavoidable extreme unction, a few final moments of sincerity were granted the dying person. Following a vague recollection of the Bible, the marranos would customarily expire facing the wall. The bizarre custom of placing a gold coin or a jewel – the price for crossing the Jordan – in the dead person's mouth was, instead, an inheritance of Greek mythology. But the ritual cleansing/washing and the days of mourning did follow Jewish norms. However much they wanted to be buried in a Jewish cemetery – and all the more so if their own family members rested there – this almost never happened.

The marranos, who had been forced to live as Christians, died as renegade Jews reciting the Shema or just murmuring the name Adonai. Yet in the grip of that lacerating conflict they maintained a sense of belonging to the community of the diaspora and did not abandon hope of liberation.

Teresa of Ávila and the Interior Castle

Over time, however, together with the Hebraizing marranos there were increasing numbers of *conversos* who accepted Christianity. At least two different, if not opposing, types emerged. Driven by a powerful grudge, some hid their belonging even to the point of repressing it among others, becoming zealous and ferociously anti-Jewish Catholics. The most lamentably famous name in this sense is Tomás de Torquemada. A pioneer of police despotism and bureaucratic tyranny, ruthless and meticulous, he introduced a theological–political use of terror, ensuring the Inquisition's properly legal character. He worked to push Christian identity at any cost. This was an identity not based in blood but rather celebrated with water and, if necessary, reinforced with fire.

Conversely, there were also *conversos* who eagerly accepted the new faith but also maintained a certain dissent – the brand of their marrano past. Rather than assimilate, they changed Christianity itself. They found a haven especially in the monasteries; for instance the one in Guadalupe. In these secluded sites, it was easier for them to explore the territory of their own interior world, avoiding Latin and the Catholic rites. In this sense they were comparable to the Hebraizing marranos. The new mysticism reached its acme in the work of a woman both anguished and ironic, radical and impassioned – a figure who escaped the limits of her era and today appears a contemporary.

But who was Teresa de Cepeda y Ahumada, proclaimed not only a saint but a Doctor of the Universal Church? To answer this question, it is necessary to turn back to an oft-overlooked story – the painful and gloomy history of the *conversos* accused of Hebraizing and publicly humiliated for this reason. When the Inquisition took up residence in Toledo in 1485, Juan Sánchez, a draper and *mercader*, was tried for 'crimes of heresy'. In the *auto da fé* that followed he was forced to pass through the streets of the city together with his wife Inés de Cepeda – a *cristiana vieja* – and their children, including six-year-old Alonso, wearing a *sambenito*, the infamous yellow scapular that marked out the marranos. For seven Fridays the 'reconciled' walked barefoot, shouldering enormous burnt-out candles and heavy crosses, amid the mockery and the invective of the crowd. After this grim ceremony, the *sambenito* was left hanging in the church with the name of the condemned person, as a marker of his unending dishonour. The family had lost its *honra* – its reputation.

Juan Sánchez left Toledo – at the time almost a metropolis – to take refuge in Ávila, a small city in the Castilian *meseta* over a thousand metres above sea level. He acquired a fake certificate of *hidalguía*, which supposedly attested to the family's 'clean' blood and thus warded off the danger of prison and torture. He continued to sell silk and wool, until he succumbed to the plague of 1507. His son Alonso tried both to overcome this terrible loss and eliminate any trace of Jewishness; in his second wedding he married Beatriz de Ahumada, who belonged to the lower nobility. On 28 March 1515 Teresa was born – so named in memory of her paternal great-grandmother Teresa Sánchez. The inconvenient Hebrew patronymic disappeared, to be replaced by Catholic surnames. Yet the Cepeda y Ahumada family would not remain above all suspicion – in 1519 a tax case was brought against them in which the inerasable past again reared its head. Could it be that the future saint knew nothing of all this? Without doubt, throughout her life she would be afflicted by the obligation to *sustentar la honra*, to bear the weight of a stigma.

Her brothers emigrated to the New World and the favourite son Rodrigo set off for the Río de la Plata. As for Teresa, in the shadow of the convent of Carmelo she worked her way through the tangled and meandering paths of the interior landscape. Decisive was the role of her uncle, Pedro de Cepeda, who, having withdrawn into silence and meditation, introduced her to the mysticism of another *converso*, Francisco de Osuna. After a journey marked by enthusiasms and slumps, illnesses and recoveries, bewilderment and zeal, in 1555 she finally arrived at what her biographers call her moment of 'conversion'. Her contemplative life intensified, while the idea of reforming the order by returning to the 'barefoot' Carmelo was also consolidated. Now began the epic pilgrimage, an itinerant journey to found one monastery after another. Yet this did not stop her writing.

What did this have to do with marranism? Did it distance her, too, from the ostentatious ceremonies and the comforts of the official religion, driving her towards an innovative interiority? This is what Michel de Certeau argues. He sets Teresa of Ávila within the radicalism of the humiliated tradition, the marrano tradition of the 'new Christians', divided souls pervaded by the need for a hidden intimacy. There were very many such outcasts – from the *beatas* to the *alumbrados,* the enlightened spirituals – exponents of an intelligentsia that found refuge in the monasteries. Their 'convert' face remained the mask of the excluded Jew. Thus, De Certeau observed: 'a strange alliance conjoins the word "mysticism" and the "impure" blood. The encounter between two religious traditions – one pushed into a withdrawal into inner life, the other triumphant but "corrupted" – allowed the new Christians to be, in large measure, the creators of a new discourse liberated from structured, dogmatic repetition, a sort of spiritual marranism, through the opposition between the "purity" within and the lie "outside".' Hence, this is why the mystics did not recoil from the ruins of corrupted Orders: rather, they entered into them in order to overhaul and restore them. Within Christianity, they articulated the experience of an elsewhere. Between meditation and poetry, it was their autobiographical journeys that allowed an unhoped-for freedom, at the limit of folly, to cross the 'dark night of the soul', as the title of Juan de la Cruz's famous poem put it.

Urged on by her confessors, Teresa of Ávila also wrote. First was the *Book of My Life*. Then the other works and, ultimately, her masterpiece *Las Moradas* – 'The Dwellings' – also known as *El Castillo interior*. The castle is an imaginary image, a 'borrowed dwelling', where the soul can let itself be transported outside itself, where that speech that has no place to make itself heard can instead find space. Her writing seemed to indulge the male authority of the *letrados*, the ecclesiastical scholars who traced its limits, revised, corrected, so that it did not transgress the Catholic framework. *Obediencia* was required. But, paradoxically, Teresa could obey only by disobeying; for her discourse – through its provenance and destination – went beyond her. It was both hers and not hers. She thus wrote in a way that responded to the demands of that shared speech coming from her circle. It unfolded in an in-between space – a space between women; in its dual difference, both feminine and marrano, it could not but infringe and contaminate the Catholic universe. Otherwise, she would have had to have stayed silent. She continued onward, nonetheless, even though she knew that the Inquisition had its eye on her, keeping her under surveillance.

In the 'enchanted castle', atopic and poetic, which in its nothingness stands opposed to the authority of the real, apocalyptic memories of the biblical Jerusalem and messianic images of the return follow one after the other. Diamond and crystal reflect the light of this interior space where the other speaks *por mí*, for me. The dialogue of the soul follows in the wake of the Socratics, but it unfolds through a doubling and an alteration: the other inhabits the self and the self the other. There is no integral identity. You are other than yourself. Even in the mystical union, the self's separation from itself is inevitable. Rather, it is thanks to the separation that the soul can host, provide space for, the infinite other. This is the discovery of the Indies of God.

One should not underestimate the political significance of the castle, a bulwark against any *auto da fé*. With its practice of uninterrupted questioning – up to and including torture – the Inquisition presumed to be able to access the most intimate and secret self, which, once uncovered, could be brought to light and punished in public. Teresa of Ávila, for her part, indicated a self inaccessible even to itself, inhabited by the other, infinitely other. This was thus a sacred self, which it was necessary to defend and safeguard. The entirety of marrano mysticism is a response to the violence of the Inquisitors.

'Válete por ti!'[7]

But was it actually necessary to choose between Judaism and Christianity and to thrash around within this painful dilemma? Many marranos – perhaps the majority – sought a further escape route and took their distance from all religion. They were the first secular Jews and in large measure (given that the Greeks were pagans) also the first atheists, daring to present themselves on the stage of history at the dawn of modernity.

To be secular does not necessarily mean to be atheist. But over the arc of time in which marranism as a phenomenon intensified, religion came to lose its previously central role. Pining for salvation in the afterlife, sacrificing one's life, enduring torments, ending up on the stake – why bother? Who had decreed this? Authority was

7 'Look after yourself' or 'Do good by yourself.'

dismissed, while the internal self became an alternative tribunal in which – before there had been any trial – the marrano could absolve herself, rejecting any faith and emancipating herself from any bondage. The extreme tension between Judaism and Christianity helped prompt a growing indifference towards religion in general. Neither Jews nor Christians, these *conversos* found an exit route precisely in this double negation, neither–nor, which, thanks to the subsequent marrano diaspora, would have decisive effects on philosophical thinking.

At that first moment, this was not a matter of deep and complex meditation. Rather, the choice was dictated by a practical opportunity, joined to a need for liberation and a compelling desire to live one's existence in this world rather than preoccupy oneself with the afterlife. This did not imply proclaiming oneself an atheist or agnostic. That was especially true given that it was indispensable to keep ideas of this kind well hidden – for the Inquisitors, they sounded even more heretical and dangerous. Not a few *conversos*, moreover, had begun to think that each had the right to follow their own faith and there were also early sparks of deism – the assertion of God's existence, on rational bases.

But the truly disruptive event was irreligiosity. The eclipse of transcendence marked the beginning of immanence. The earthly world, between birth and death, became the only arena in which each person could test their own capacities, taking their chances.

As one *converso* facing the Inquisition summarized his new creed, 'There is no paradise other than the market of Calatayud.' And this creed was also echoed in other reports. A certain Juan López cockily stated 'Say what you like, there is no God other than money.' Another, Gonzalo del Rincón, gave his blunt judgement: 'Don't you see? The only law that counts in this world is profit: whoever *has* is respected, whoever *hasn't* is marginalized.' Though here one must inevitably highlight the stereotype of the Jew who worships money rather than pray to God, all the same, these accounts do document a tendency that was now asserting itself – an ever more pronounced tendency for the realization of the individual, his own career and his own success.

If in one etymological sense 'religion' means 'bringing together', 'uniting', one of the causes of irreligiosity was the decline of the bonds of tradition, which also owed to the fragmentation of communities. The secularized and immanentist marrano was, at root, doing nothing other than acknowledge this new existence in which, torn from his tradition and unable to integrate himself into another, he was instead left up to himself, to his own judgement and his own choices. Solitude, mournfulness and discomfort obfuscated a universe agitated by powerful forces. Such is the universe that shines through from the tragicomedy *La Celestina*, attributed to the *converso* Fernando de Rojas and published anonymously in 1499. Only erotic passion seemed still able to retain some sense of the unquenchable, in a world condemned to remain unredeemed.

Nonetheless, it was *Lazarillo de Tormes* – the marrano child, the child marrano – who immortalized the tough experiences of the Spanish *conversos*. The archetype of picaresque literature, whose unprecedented biographical form reflected the only recently discovered interior self, the novel appeared anonymously in Burgos in 1554 and was banned by the Inquisition in 1559. The protagonist is not a knight or a hero. Rather, he is an anti-hero, bathed in neither honour nor nobility. He could, perhaps, be counted among the *pícaros* – those cunning common rascals who have had to learn to get by on their own through schemes and swindles. Yet Lazarillo is different from them, too. Orphan to a father who 'suffered persecutions by the justice system', *por la justicia*, and abandoned by a much gossiped-about mother, the lover to a Moor, the child passes from one master to another – a blind man, a priest, a squire – and fights only for survival, amid hunger, beatings and exploitation. Using an ironic, even if crude, allusive and almost esoteric register, the novel captures Lázaro's desperate cry and articulates the resigned injunction coming from his mother, both a protest and a denunciation: *válete por ti*. 'Son, I know that I will not see you any more. Try to be good and may God help you. I have raised you and found you a good master: now you must find your worth for yourself.'

Lazarillo's path continues without his mother, without community and without tradition.

An Insult and its Fantastic History

Doubtless, 'marrano' is a pejorative word. But from where did such a bizarre term originate? Countless hypotheses have been advanced, in this regard: from the Castilian *marrar*, to wander, to the Aramaic *marantha*, an excommunicated person, from the Hebrew wordplay of *mar* (bitter) and *anus* (convert) to the Arabic *mura'in*, hypocrite, or *barran*, foreigner, or finally *mahram*, something prohibited. This last etymology seems the most widely credited. But the lucubrations could continue.

This much is certain, at least: the Spanish term marrano was used as a synonym for pig, in order to stigmatize, taunt and wound the *conversos*. This insult, which must have circulated already previously, was subsequently used for the Jews who were forcibly baptized, who remained perfidious and treacherous. A marrano was a *maldito, sin fe* – damned and without faith. But in the terrible insult against the converted evil – equated with the *cerdo,* the pig – further accusations and implied threats also resonated.

For those looking from the outside, the Jews' abstinence from pig meat – following a biblical precept – must have appeared as their most striking trait. But this trait was turned into a stigma, as if to say: 'you who consider yourselves pure because you do not eat the impure animal, are yourselves mere pigs'. The zoologization of the human was, sadly, already a widespread practice. These foul people of Jewish faith, who contaminated and stained the pure, legitimate Christians, were characterized as *cerdos* more than as dogs, monkeys or other animals. And by Hebraizing – that is, by maintaining ancient Jewish habits, even if this just meant repugnance for that meat – they contaminated Christians. That is how one could recognize a *converso* and unmask a marrano. It was pointless to add that getting rid of such foul beasts would not, therefore, be all that difficult.

The popular scorn spread to such a degree that in 1380 John I of Castile banned it, upon pain of being fined or jailed. Clearly, 'marrano' must have been a serious insult. But there was little point to this ban. While this term did not appear in laws and official documents, which preferred to speak of *conversos*, *confesos* or *cristianos nuevos*, this was only because they feigned neutrality even as they decreed extermination.

The term then emigrated from the Iberian Peninsula, chasing after the new Christians in the diaspora. However, being too exotic it did not enjoy much success in other countries, with the exception of Italy, where its first and no-longer-transparent meaning ('unclean') soon spread. The insult endured as a stamp for those converts who were neither Jews nor Christians, but only – indeed – *marrani*. That is what the common people, chroniclers, historians, even philosophers and writers called them: such was the case of Machiavelli in his *The Prince* (XXI). At this point, 'marrano' also took on a different meaning: a traitor, a liar, a heretic. For the Italians – with their propensity not to overdramatize matters of faith and morality – this was not ever so serious. Ironically, this utterly Spanish word was extended to refer to the Spaniards themselves, who were unable to make peace with it. The very people who had taken such trouble to castigate the real marranos, monitoring them with holy Inquisitors and burning people at the stake, were put in the same basket as them! Once the acrimony against the Spanish oppressors had worn thin, in Italy the term 'marrano' indicated only the traitor, liar and villain, the 'mancator di fé', as the verses of Ariosto put it. Thus, in epic-chivalrous poems, the marrano was he who did not respect the laws of courtesy and keep promises; he was the uncouth, the villain, the '*vil* marrano' – an insult that the *condottiero* Francesco Ferrucci directed against the captain of fortune Fabrizio Maramaldo, before he was himself ignobly killed. That is why the term, in its various forms, including the interjection '*marameo!*' – 'don't do this to me!', 'don't trick me!' – could also be directed at a rebellious child. This explains the difference between Italian, on the one hand, and Spanish and Portuguese, on the other, where the still-blatantly offensive term 'marrano' is rejected.

If up to a few years ago the prevalent term in Italian was 'crypto-Jews' – a form of words that seemed more politically correct – today 'marrano' has again become more common. Perhaps this unconsciously respects the assertion so proudly made by Roth, when he wrote that '[t]he word ["marrano"] expresses succinctly and unmistakably all the depth of hatred and contempt that the ordinary Spaniard felt for the insincere neophytes by whom he was now surrounded. It is the constancy shown by them and their descendants that has redeemed the term from its former insulting connotation and endowed it with its enduring power of romance.'[8]

The Planetary Archipelago and the Anarchic Nation

Right from the years that followed the great expulsion, the marranos tried to escape by land and, above all, by sea. Yet one decree after another threw up obstacles to their departure: it was held that their souls would go astray, or – and perhaps this was a more pressing

8 Cecil Roth, *A History of the Marranos*, Varda Books, Skokie, IL, 2001 [1932], p. 28.

reason – they ran the risk of their assets being confiscated. Nonetheless, the accounts of the time describe the Iberian ports as overflowing with marrano refugees ready to board the first vessel to reach the coasts of North Africa, the cities of Italy or, best of all, the Ottoman Empire, where they could have openly returned to Judaism.

Thus began the marrano diaspora, which continued for a full three centuries, reaching its peak around 1680. Over time, their routes multiplied and their destinations became ever more remote, uncertain and extreme. It was no longer only a matter of the Mediterranean or the North Sea. They set off from Lisbon and Seville towards the two Indies – both East and West – in the European imagination representing the fabled escape routes to the New World. And what more did they have to fear, after all that they had already suffered? Alongside the need for freedom there was the quest for another life, the desire for more opportunities, but also a certain spirit of adventure – an irrepressible, nervous enthusiasm to explore the unknown. Were there not, perhaps, marranos on the first explorers' ships? On Christopher Columbus' voyage, even? The discovery of America was in large part a marrano endeavour. For it had been the Aragonese *conversos* who had taken seriously the half-messianic dream of this unique Genoese explorer, rumoured himself to be Jewish. And on the caravels there were no few Judaizers: Alonso de la Calle, Rodrigo Sanchez, Mestre

Bernal and one Luis de Torres, the interpreter on board. The first to set foot on American soil, he perhaps tried out his Hebrew on the native *indios*.

Vast distances were travelled and the most remote borders were crossed. Merchants and martyrs, rabbis and poets, doctors and adventurers, explorers and revolutionaries, dreamers and heretics, they were the protagonists of an epochal adventure, a journey into the unlimited, from which a dense web of connections developed. Venice and Antwerp, Thessaloniki and Madeira, Bordeaux and Curaçao – ships came and went from one port to another at ever-accelerating rhythms. Soon bays and harbours in Brazil also became accessible, whence spun out two further routes. One followed the Venezuelan coast in the direction of the Caribbean islands. The other, which was tougher and riskier, passed up the Río de la Plata out toward the boundless plains of Argentina. Along this route it was possible to cross through the landscapes of the Amazon and reach the legendary city of Potosí. Each connection was followed by another. One emblematic date was 1570, when the first ships setting off from Macao – an overseas Portuguese province – approached the port in the Spanish colony of Manila. One could say that an initial form of globalization had now been achieved.

However, in this period, at the dawn of modernity, contacts remained sporadic and fragmented. There was nothing to protect against the myriad threats that accompanied every crossing and the dangers of every expedition. Capital, with its anonymous power and its rules of exchange, did not yet exist – there was no system of guarantees. What could stop the addressee appropriating the goods with impunity upon delivery? If there was a shipwreck, who would compensate for the losses? While long-distance trade brought lucrative profits, it was also enormously risky. The marranos, who were often owners of the ships or the cargoes, sorted the products. In Genoa, as in other ports, from Hamburg to Livorno, they sold silk, oil, wine, herring, wheat, dried fruits, and bought sugar, cocoa, tobacco, spices and diamonds imported by the East India Company. Some of them were involved in the incipient slave traffic as well as piratical operations. In this, they followed a widespread idea of trade, which, outside European borders, escaped any morality.

How, then, could merchants at thousands of miles' distance properly conclude an exchange, when they did not know each other and had perhaps never seen each other? While others did not have credit, the marranos – enveloped in suspicion and diffidence, accused of being cheats – had needed to learn to trust each other. Mutual trust, the precious legacy of a fraternal bond developed under forced clandestinity, thus allowed for an extraordinary web of connections. This did not mean that no conflicts cropped up, or that cons and fraud could be ruled out. But what prevailed, above all, was solidarity, something all the more necessary given that the Inquisitors had not given up their exhausting pursuit. However, the marranos had brought with them their multiple names and the now-consolidated practice of a sudden shift from one identity to another. Moshe Abensur circulated through the Baltic ports under the name Paulo Millão, Abraham Isaac under the name Diogo Teixeira, and Michael Beira under the name Luis Franco. Thus not a few of them were even able to return to Iberia. How could they be identified? For them, too, alternating between one name and another had become a habit, without the Hebrew, Spanish or Portuguese one imposing itself over the others. A *converso* from Toulouse could turn to a Judaizer from Ancona, a freethinker from London or a new Christian from Antwerp, convinced that his letter would be understood and his request for the most part satisfied. This web of ties was heterogeneous and thus was able to integrate very different individuals, with their tangled histories and tormented choices.

The word 'diaspora', adopted from Hebrew history, does not correspond to the dispersion of the marranos. The diaspora has a centre around which it rotates. However powerful the myth of the old Sepharad may have remained across the centuries, this land was certainly not the place to which the marranos aspired to return. Their movements were centrifugal, their routes multiple and varied. Yovel has suggested the image of a constellation: over the decades, some stars (Antwerp, Ferrara, Dutch Brazil) faded whereas others (Amsterdam, Livorno, Thessaloniki) shone all the more brilliantly, followed by countless satellites and comets. But the metaphor of the archipelago seems even more fitting: that is, scattered islands, both divided and connected by the sea, which display ever-differing similarities among themselves. What could marranos who lived in Germany or in Mexico, in Bulgaria or the Bahamas, in Damascus or Buenos Aires, have in common? They spoke Portuguese, they wrote in Spanish, they knew a little Italian, they remembered a few words of Hebrew. They were modernity's first migrants, destined no longer to have a homeland of their own. Just as their self was split, they would be forever separated from any place.

Yet the marrano archipelago also earned itself a name. In Portuguese it was called the *Nação*. The etymology of 'nation' refers to birth, indicating a common origin. Long before it was bent to nationalist aims, the term was used in Italy's universities in order to distinguish between students: those from Padua, Siena, Urbino, Naples and other cities. The merchant colonies in the trading hubs were similarly designated, from Bruges to Hamburg and Genoa. In a document signed Antwerp, 1511, there appeared for the first time the formula 'Portuguese nation'. This was a licence granted to Lisbon merchants, Hebraizing 'new Christians'. This formulation, which was perhaps already widespread in this period, then cropped up ever more frequently, with certain variations: the 'Spanish and Portuguese nation', 'Portuguese of the Jewish nation', 'Portuguese of the Nation', 'people of the Nation' or more simply, *Nação*. The terms 'Portuguese' and 'Jewish' overlapped to the point of becoming synonymous – proof that, as others saw things, Portuguese were considered marranos. But what could a word like *Nação* really mean?

The *Nação* had emerged before the establishment of nation-states. In its broad extension, which did not coincide with the Jewish people itself, it represented an unprecedented political form, in many ways eccentric and paradoxical. Not only did it not exhibit the structure of a state, but nor could it lay claim to a territory, to borders. On the contrary, the members of the *Nação* were scattered across the four corners of the world. Dispersion and mobility were, therefore, their characteristic traits. It is impossible to say who commanded sovereignty and where this sovereignty was based. Rather, though the *Nação* remained united, it did not have a sovereign. There were those, here and there, who temporarily advised, kept watch and gave instructions, but this was a *Nação* of an anarchist stamp.

Its members were linked by bonds that were anything but self-evident. Birth was not an important criterion, here, since not all of them still came from the Iberian Peninsula – they were born elsewhere. They could not vaunt any ethnic line of descent, for they were well aware that they had mixed with Spaniards, the Portuguese, Italians, the Dutch, the English and, gradually, with all the peoples with whom they lived. They considered themselves to be members of the *Nação* not out of some identitarian bond, which they did not in fact have. Rather, they considered themselves its members because of the stigma that had made them the other's other – the suspicion that had everywhere pursued them. It was history that brought them together and the memory of their secret, which did not abandon them, whatever their multiple differences. Crypto-Jews, new Christians, or agnostics, they were all residents of a varied archipelago. And though the marranos were also called *homens de negócios*, this archipelago was not limited to a well-functioning global trade network.

Precious testimony to this fact appears in the statutes, drawn up in 1615, of an Amsterdam confraternity known as the Santa Companhia de dotar orfans e donzelas pobres. Its purpose was to assist the orphans of the *Nação* and, in particular, poor girls living in Saint-Jean-de-Luz, in Danzig and in other cities, without geographical limits. This also extended to places where the intended recipients of aid had needed to become new Christians, for survival's sake. The criterion for aid was not, therefore, *halakha* – observance of the precepts – but rather a secret fidelity. It was enough to have 'belief in the Unity of the Lord of the World and the knowledge of the Most Holy Law, whether or not they are circumcized and whether or not they live within Judaism'. Their duty was to uphold the memory of a single God and of a law that survived even when not practised. The marranos were Jewish because of a remembrance anchored to the future, divided between rites, traditions and languages. They were resident foreigners, in exile everywhere across the archipelago. And they were united in the *Nação* – the first global messianic project.

The 'New Jews', between Livorno and Amsterdam

Having come out of the 'land of idolatry', after unspeakable pain and terrible suffering, the marranos could return to the faith of their fathers. Thus they came back to Western Europe, which had hardly any Jewish residents in the early 1500s. England had expelled them in 1290, France in 1306 and again in 1394, as had Germany over the course of the last century. Several Italian cities had also done the same. Slowly, new communities took form and old ones revived. This provided the context in which a both peculiar and unexpected phenomenon emerged. The marranos, who had so long lived in Iberian exile, keeping faith with the Mosaic law, became 'new Jews'. They had already been 'new Christians'; again now, they were certainly 'new'. But were they Jewish?

The impact was traumatic. These Jews were true

idolators – without knowing it. And once they became aware of this, their reaction was unpredictable. Some decided to remain Christians, while others took remedial action by learning Hebrew and studying the Talmud. Others were attracted to the community but put off by the observance of the precepts. Yet others 'marranized'. Such was what happened in Venice: one day they were in the ghetto with the other Jews, one day they were outside, mixed in among the Christians.

Henceforth, the new Jews looked on from the outside at the Jewish tradition, which thus seemed interrupted and broken. It was no longer that homogeneous ground in which they could feel always already included. Inevitably, everything that they had learned over the course of years and decades – that which they had, perhaps even unconsciously, become – had its own repercussions. This critical eye itself, with which they had learned to scrutinize themselves within, was turned to the outside, almost as if to decide whether to accept this tradition or to reject it, in what measure and in what way. This unfamiliarity did not disappear with their return – it had only changed direction. The new Jews, these old marranos, discovered that they had become inexorably modern.

A specular marranism took form, this time tearing the Jewish world apart. The rabbis were overwhelmed by questions and puzzlement of all kinds, which they struggled to deal with, while the *parnassim*, the secular leaders, became unwilling to bear the ambivalence that was now jeopardizing the community. Tacit dissent was still tolerated; but open dissent, however conceptual, could not but sound like a challenge. The victims were intellectuals, freethinkers, philosophers like Gabriel (Uriel) Costa, Juan (Daniel) de Prado and Baruch Spinoza. If Prado was the first non-orthodox Jew, Spinoza elevated the marranos' resistance to a philosophical category.

The repercussions were, obviously, varied, across different places and circumstances. While accounts from the time report that there was not a single city in Italy that had not seen large numbers of 'Portuguese' amassing, at first it was above all Ferrara that opened its doors to the refugees. Starting in 1530 it thus became a chosen destination for the marranos, who could freely return to Judaism; later, however, when the pressure of the Counter-Reformation began to make itself felt, all liberties were abolished. Many marranos were thrown into prison. In 1583 three of them, considered the guiltiest, were sent to Rome for an *auto da fé*. The Inquisition put them to death and decided to burn them at the stake. Joseph (Abraham) Saralbo, alias Gabriel Henriques, bravely passed through the narrow city streets without letting his head down. He was remembered as a martyr. They burned in that same Campo de' Fiori where Giordano Bruno would be burnt alive just a few years later. Yet there is no stone to remember them.

Whereas in Venice – among many ins and outs – the coexistence of Italian, Ashkenazi and Sephardic Jews gave rise to a multifaceted community, Livorno was the marrano city *par excellence*. This owed not only to the so-called *Livornina*, the 1591 document in which the grand duke of Tuscany welcomed the new immigrants, but also to the fact that this city had no existing community and, most importantly, no ghetto. The marranos thus impressed a character of openness and freedom across the city.

It is not known how many marranos reached the banks of the river Amstel. But already at the beginning of the seventeenth century, Amsterdam had become the 'Jerusalem of the North'. Thousands of people facing persecution had found refuge there. The city was repaid for this generous hospitality – on land reclaimed from the water – with an unexpected golden age, becoming a cosmopolitan metropolis. Trade prospered, exchange multiplied and the arts flourished. The Sephardis, who had recovered their freedom of worship, were very soon considered the Jewish elite of Europe. Rembrandt immortalized them in his paintings, as refined, melancholy and proud. These are, fundamentally, the few remaining images of the marranos. One particularly prominent one is the portrait of Menasseh ben Israel, the troubled rabbi. Together with the painter, he shared a vision with a strong messianic inspiration.

Messianic Sparks

The expulsion must have produced a trauma similar to that which followed Auschwitz. The catastrophe seemed all the graver on account of the conversion of so many *annusim*, an enormous loss to the Jewish people. There was such disorientation as to shake centuries-old principles. It was necessary to shed light on those ark events and, amid that historic night, try to make out the dawn of a new liberation.

What Gershom Scholem has called the 'great myth of exile' thus developed. The anxious concern to decipher this enigma had repercussions even on mysticism itself. The Kabbalah was conjugated with messianism and opened up – like never before – to wide layers of the population. Having been an origin myth, directed at explaining a creation permeated with apocalyptic themes, it was now turned towards interpreting the end. Everything was reconsidered in light of exile. Even the creation was but the exile of God, withdrawing in order to take up a place in the world. From this great cosmic drama, from this original rupture, from this dispersion of divine sparks, the reparation could play out. Only exile would allow the return. A shift took place, from cosmology to politics. Indeed, messianism – which had constituted the crossing point for conversion – was recuperated and launched afresh, in a new philosophy of history. Isaac Abravanel was first to recount, indeed

in epochal tones, an event through which he himself
had lived:

> The people heard this terrible news [the expulsion
> edict]: everywhere the King's word and his decree
> reached, there was a great sorrow ... And three hun-
> dred thousand people set off from all the King's
> provinces on a single day, unarmed and on foot,
> elements of that people of which I am myself part –
> young and old, women and children. Some reached
> the Kingdoms of Portugal and Navarra, which are
> closest, only to find dark misery and endless woes.
> They were prey to numerous and cruel tests, of pillage
> and destruction, of hunger and plagues. Others took
> the sea route and journeyed across perilous waters.
> There, too, the hand of the Eternal came down on
> them, giving them up and destroying them. For
> many of our children were abandoned to desolation
> and sold as slaves and serfs in all the Gentile lands.
> Many drowned in the sea, draining into the powerful
> waters like lead. Still others passed through fire and
> water because the boats burned and the flame of the
> Eternal raged against them.

Nonetheless, Abravanel did not stop at recounting these
events. Rather, in a messianic trilogy written between
1496 and 1498 he pointed to the extreme misfortune –
this apocalyptic end – as the beginning of the liberation
of the oppressed and the exiled. The time had come.

But first, messianism would have to become a universal inheritance. This is why the dispersion was necessary.

Menasseh ben Israel further picked up this theme in his book *The Hope of Israel*, published in 1650. Already, bewildering news had arrived from the other side of the Atlantic. Returning from the Americas in 1642, Antonio de Montezinos, alias Aaron Levi, claimed that he had come across *indios* who recited the Shema, the Jewish prayer. They were, it was thought, descendants of the tribe of Reuben. Here was the much-awaited proof: the Jewish diaspora had reached every corner of the planet. This was the sign of imminent messianic times. This discovery in the New World was the pretext to announce the Jews' return to the Old World, which had converted to the nation-state, where – as the experience of the marranos had shown – there had no longer seemed to be any place for them. But they returned in order to change its political landscape.

The path indicated by Menasseh was already turned to the outside world. But the adventure of the pseudo-Messiah Sabbatai Zevi – awakening a messianic excitement that agitated and troubled the communities of Europe and the Mediterranean – was, instead, wholly internal to Judaism. His conversion to Islam and then death provoked enormous upset. But messianism remained a peculiar trait of the marrano world and was certainly the source of radical political thinking.

Spinoza, Democracy, the Freedom of the Secret

On 27 July 1656 Bento Spinoza, registered under the Jewish name Baruch, was expelled from Amsterdam's Jewish community. He was twenty-four years of age. The ban or *cherem* was read in the Houtgracht synagogue by the *parnassim* gathered in the *Ma'amad*, the council made up of the secular authorities. The circumstances and reasons behind the *cherem* remain in many regards enigmatic. This is also cause for the fascination exerted by Spinoza as a figure, by his history and by his thought. When he decided to leave Amsterdam in 1660, this produced an irreparable split, which sanctioned the beginning of the modern era. Spinoza was not only the first secular Jew, but also the first intellectual of secularized modernity. Unlike other dissidents and heretics like Uriel da Costa who chose to stay within the Jewish community or to pass over to another religion, Spinoza ventured into the terra incognita of secularization. Far from rabbinical Judaism, he did not abandon the 'Jewish nation' in exile. He still considered himself – and was considered – Jewish. This had inevitable repercussions on the manner in which Jewish identity was understood.

Personally involved in the Sephardic diaspora, and coming from an oppressed and persecuted Portuguese family, Spinoza introduced marranism into the thought of Western modernity. Who other than a marrano could have radically conceived of democracy in its indissoluble link with freedom? The *Theological-Political Treatise* was a charge-sheet against totalizing power – that power exercised over bodies, which, moreover, seeks to control ideas, scope intentions and suss out the most intimate secrets. And speaking, here, was not the rising star of *Keter Torah*, the Talmudic school, or still less an accursed heretic, but rather the son of crypto-Jews who had returned to freedom.

What, then, did Spinoza write in the solitude of Voorburg? He beat a course back to the setting that had underpinned, and still underpinned, the marranos' hope: the story of the exodus. Finally liberated from the 'intolerable oppression of the Egyptians', no longer slaves, the Jews reconquered their rights. They could decide whether to cede them to a sovereign, as the other peoples had done. Instead, they chose 'to transfer their right to no mortal man but rather to God alone'.[9] And, without hesitating, with one voice, *all equally with one shout*, they promised. They bound themselves with a covenant, 'freely, not compelled by force, or frightened by threats'. So long as that pact should be 'accepted and settled without any suspicion of fraud', God made no agreement until the Jews 'had experienced his astound-

9 Baruch Spinoza, *Theological-Political Treatise*, Cambridge University Press, Cambridge, 2007, p. 213.

ing power'. Thus, the subversive God of the exodus brought out his people with a clenched fist and an arm outstretched: 'I carried you on eagles' wings and brought you to myself.'[10] It was because they believed that they could save themselves also in the future that the Jews entrusted 'all their right' to God. The result was a theocracy, God's exclusive government.

But it lasted only a moment – the time for the Jews to make the promise and, through that theological-political pact, to constitute themselves as a people. In that cry, God's government dissipated. The people, however, continued to be free – unlike those subjects who had chosen a monarch. What, then, remained after that moment? What remained was a new political form, based on the equality of all – democracy. This did not mean that hybrid power upheld by the Greeks, which is to say, a merely quantitative extension of monarchy, which hid the slavery going on around its edges. Aristotle justified that as natural. But there was to be none of all this. Rather, democracy – something unknown to the classical world – is introduced by exodus. The form is the same: in democracy's case, the right first transferred to God is instead transferred to reason. Slavery cannot be accepted. For the legacy of this exemplary passage is that no one can be enslaved to her equal. Democracy demands equality and gives rise

10 Exodus, 19, 4.

to a community that can extend to become a universal assembly.

A manifesto for a liberation of the marranos, the *Theological-Political Treatise* closes with a famous appeal – a call necessary for the advent of democracy itself. Here, Spinoza writes that 'no soul can be subjected to the right of others'. Hence 'a power exercised over souls must be considered violent'. One cannot 'prescribe to others what to accept as true or reject as false'. It is pointless to want to control and submit others through fear. And he calls for freedom, of thought as of speech. But he also calls for the right to 'secrecy'. Remembering the drama that the marranos had experienced, he intuited that only the inaccessible space of the secret could hinder the totalitarian power of the publicness that ensnares democracy.

The Political Laboratory of Modernity

It is no accident that marranism emerged with such disruptive force at the dawn of modernity. It is as if the Jews expelled in 1492 and the marranos who subsequently fled during the great dispersion, were, against their own intentions, cast out of the Middle Ages and projected into a new era. The marrano becomes the matrix of the modern Jew in her multiple figures. The question is no longer 'what should I do?' – the problem that has for centuries followed Jews, daily reminded of the heteronomy of the commandments. Rather, the marrano watching herself in the scrutinizing gaze of the other asks herself 'who am I?' The lacerated consciousness of the modern Jew, her anguished back and forth between insertion and marginality, derives from the marrano split.

Marranism repeats its steps. This compels us to consider it a phenomenon much wider and deeper than is generally believed. It is no longer possible to think of it only as a condition to which people are subjected, only the result of violence and coercion. How, then, could it have permeated personal biographies, travelled across the years and decades up till modernity? How could it have arisen in an identity considered as strong as Jewish identity? That is why Shmuel Trigano has spoken of a 'marrano syndrome in Judaism'. This syndrome lies in the fracture in the essential unity between an outside and a within – a fracture that emerges in exceptional biblical figures, first of all Esther. But then also Joseph. The secret conceals a hidden messianic potential, while its betrayal turns into salvation. The gesture repeats itself, to the point that the history of the marranos, in all its gravity, brings to light the Jews' propensity to marranism. Imposed by force, marranism also reveals itself to be an act of courage, capable of ensuring the survival of the Jewish people, despite the risk of collapse and extinction. How would it be possible to explain the marranos' perseverance in this unconfessable secret of theirs, up to the moment of return, if not in terms of this propensity? Marranism is inscribed in Judaism from the origin. To put that another way: the origin of Judaism is marrano.

Seen in this light, the emancipation of the Jews appears as a reiteration of marranism – this time, however, it is something rationally embraced rather than imposed through violence. Now it is single individuals that are 'emancipated', not the people. Having become a citizen, the modern Jew is driven to leave behind the history, tradition and ties of belonging, and called on to melt into the abstraction of the state. The response is contained in Moses Mendelssohn's *Jerusalem*: 'Be a Jew in private and a citizen in public.' Is this not, perhaps, a marrano profession of faith? Anticipating this compromise, the marranos ceded to being 'new Christians' in public and Jews in the intimacy of the home. The decisive difference is that, having become citizens, they acquire the right to be Jews in private. This is a fundamental right, of course, which ought to guarantee freedom and equality. At the price, however, of reducing Judaism to a religion, separate from the people itself and lacking any political form. Is this enough?

The citizens of 'Mosaic confession' would still be suspected of Hebraizing in secret – the famous 'global Jewish plot' – and of perpetuating themselves as a global people, across national bounds. And, just as, despite their baptism, the 'new Christians' continued to be discriminated against – accused of having 'impure Jewish blood' – so, too, did those European citizens, so assimilated as to no longer even feel Jewish, end up being unloaded from the trains at the Nazi camps. Nor can it be said that this antisemitism has disappeared with democracy.

The Spanish monarchy's elimination of the Jews in the aftermath of the *Reconquista* can itself be considered the immediate outcome of *raison d'état*. Certainly, the subject was not a citizen. But the modern nation-state, which first took the form of absolute monarchy, required national integration. At any price. This split between public and private – something which it was the marranos' fate to experience before anyone else – represents something more. It is the model of all political modernity. Karl Marx well understood this. In his text on *The Jewish Question*, he pointed an accusing finger against the condition of the citizen, divided between public and private. In a political light, he was supposed to be equal to any other, but privately, in the sphere of the *oikos* and the economy, he was condemned to inequality. Hence the disapproval, the negative judgement Marx expressed against liberal democracy: the abstract equality it offers is but a deceptive screen that hides the lack of economic parity.

Here Marx seems to pick up on the paradoxes in which the marrano finds herself caught. What emerges above all else is alienation. If marranism is the paradigm that has left its mark on political modernity, this modernity has, in turn, been driven by the attempt to free itself of any marrano residue, to overcome alienation in order to finally rediscover its unity. But is it possible to shake off marranism? And is it really necessary to reject all dissonance, in the perspective of completion and completeness? There is nothing to say that politics must be the site of the total apparition of the human – all the more so if this is taken to mean the exteriority commanded by the state, which would then be the sole principle for ordering and articulating humanity. The marranos stood opposed to this.

Marranism in the Third Reich

If the marrano is a paradigm that goes beyond Iberian borders, is it possible to find analogous phenomena also in subsequent eras? Would such a bid, perhaps, be rather hazardous? The answer comes from Baer, among the first to reconstruct the experiences of the Sephardi Jews. In a short and touching book published in Berlin in the black year that was 1936, tellingly entitled *Galut* [exile], Baer writes: 'The marranos of those times in many aspects resemble the Jews of the Western Europe of this era.' He was sounding the alarm a year after the Nuremberg Laws, at a moment when any hope had now disappeared. The 'Jewish question in Spain', Baer continued to warn, 'teaches the modern observer that history's conflicts reproduce themselves in ever-new forms.'

Likewise, in Germany, assimilation – in various ways, without compulsion or the threat of death – had produced a multitude of marranos. What would happen to them? No one yet foresaw what would soon become the final solution to the 'Jewish question'. Yet there is something rather perturbing in the sudden, acute awakening of interest in the marranos. In 1937 the Jewish Museum in Berlin had prepared a great exhibition dedicated to Abravanel, five hundred years after his birth, in order to remember this exemplary figure and the courage with which he had fought the Holy Office, denouncing the violence of the Inquisition. The debate spread among Jewish communities and involved many intellectuals, some of whom had already emigrated, from Abraham Heschel to Leo Strauss. But it was a Dutch Jew, Valeri Marcu, who – in a book on the Jews' expulsion from Spain, published in Amsterdam in 1934 – offered a great, almost epic portrait of Abravanel, making him the pioneer of tolerance who had fought to avoid the special laws against the Jews based on 'blood purity'. Unsurprisingly, Abravanel very soon became a symbol. From French exile, Marcu sent a copy of his book to Ernst Jünger, one of the most visible writers in the Reich. But reaction instead came from Carl Schmitt, the jurist who had actively contributed to the Nuremberg Laws. In his 1942 essay *Land and Sea*, Abravanel became a bloodthirsty kabbalist. How could one do other than protect the 'blood' of the German people?

The almost morbid interest in marranism thus arose at a moment when, now on the edge of the abyss decreed by the blood laws, the European Jews discovered that they were a new type of marranos – yet still, despite everything, marranos. With growing anguish they pres-aged the end, without being able to glimpse its horrors, and turned back to reconsider the past, grasping the correspondences and parallels that they had overlooked, which they had not wanted to see.

Beyond what Yerushalmi calls 'phenomenologi-cal similarities', there was a historical continuity. It is enough to cite the words of Fritz Heymann from a 1940 lecture on the marranos, two years before he was deported to Auschwitz. He commented that: 'Some thousands of their descendants live here in Amsterdam. Yet we today, epigones of those marranos, know very little about them.' The accelerated course of events swept the dust off the archival documents, casting them in a sinister and foreboding light. What had happened before could repeat itself. For the descendants of the 'new Jews' who had escaped the Inquisition, history reserved a terrible epilogue.

This was not, then, only a matter of an old schema that re-asserted itself centuries later (even admitting all the necessary distinctions). Doubtless it is disconcerting that, after the Jews were forced with all possible means to integrate into Christianity, to melt into the political body of the nation, then, having assimilated and become similar to the point of no longer being recognizable, a renewed discrimination was launched against them, based on blood and sanctioned by state laws. Politics took recourse to theology and theology to politics. The bind was tightened. Indeed, the terms of the schema do not change even as assimilation becomes ever more secular. If Spanish antisemitism had a religious matrix, one ought not to underestimate the succession of striking cases of conversion within the German Jewish community.

In the circle of Edmund Husserl – founder of phenomenology and himself a converted Jew – Adolf Reinach, Max Scheler, Hedwig Conrad Martinus and Edith Stein chose baptism. The list could go on, including also other names, philosophers (especially female ones) who headed off to the convent. For Martius and Stein, the decisive book was Teresa of Ávila's autobiography. Not a few women converts preferred the Carmelo. This would not save them from extermination. How can these conversions – subject to so little reflection – be explained? This is a red-hot theme – and a divisive one. Stein took the name Teresa, without knowing that she was inspired by a marrana. After secluding herself in the convent of the Carmelites – a small cage in the big cage that Germany had become for the Jews – she ended up at Auschwitz. As Günther Anders has written, her last journey, in the veil of a Carmelite nun, was 'all the more excruciating than it was for the others, the thousands of human beings with whom she headed to the crematory ovens'. Under the veil remained the dark and treacherous unfamiliarity from which, as the Nazi design saw it, it was legitimate to seek protection with a pre-emptive annihilation. Thus returned the history of Esther, with the most tragic end that could be imagined.

The Counter-History of the Defeated and the Revenge of the Marranos

The global succession of events does not follow any linear, gradual, progressive course. On the contrary, history is marked by unexpected accelerations and immense ruptures. Everything seems to begin over again. Dramatic and disconcerting as they are, catastrophes do not only open up bottomless pits, depressions and abysses from which there is no recovery. And the same goes for the histories of individuals. From the depths emerges an upheaval that is simultaneously a re-reading of both the past and the future. In this sense, one can speak of a 'return'. In its intensity it does not recapitulate or restore – but it does mark a turning point.

Marranism flowered from one of these cracks. Hence its character, which distinguishes it from the outset – one proper to the catacombs. Like other phenomena that have taken place in catacombs, neither has the complicated, tortuous, cryptic experience of the marranos found a place in institutional history. Only a few illustrious cases, shorn of their marrano masks, have been able to have a voice. Still under surveillance, enveloped in silence, the marranos belong to a counter-history of the defeated. This counter-history is, in large part, still to be written and, in large part, irrecoverable. For the most part, nothing is left of these lives, their bitter vicissitudes and their tragic fates, apart from the documents conserved in the archives of the Inquisition. They are handwritten, if not with resentment, at least with the bureaucratic coldness of their enemies, who thus provide only a partial and deformed image of them. The precious contributions of scholars like Nathan Wachtel, who have delved into that subterranean world of prisons and torments, provide but discontinuous traces, segments of life torn from immense pits of darkness. They are only scattered tiles of a missing mosaic.

Yet the marranos would have their revenge. This was not only because they did not accept total defeat and remained faithful to their secret. But also because, through their varied and wandering misfortunes, marranism has reiterated itself, displaying an undeniable persistence. This is the sense in which the marranos steered clear of the archives – and remained anarchivable. This poses the need to go beyond the historiographical landscape and look at this as a phenomenon also relevant in the present.

How many marranos still exist? How many know they are marranos and have always known it, and how many are so well hidden that they don't know it or, rather, have never even suspected as much? And who can say that they are not a marrano?

'The Marrano is a Spectre I Love'

Jewish figures and themes have appeared in Jacques Derrida's thinking since the 1960s. One need only recall his essay 'Ellipsis' and that on the poetry of Edmond Jabès, each of which is included in his collection *Writing and Difference*. Both texts end with a signature – in one case, 'Reb Derissa', in the other, 'Reb Rida'. These are not the names of imaginary rabbis. Adopted from Jabès, who had inserted them among his verses as a provocation, they dissemble and deform the philosopher's own name. Rida literally cuts through – circumcizes – the name Derrida, alluding to the wound of Jewish belonging, a pact signed with a cut. Only much later, however, when *Circumfession* was published in 1991, did the theme of Judaism make its breakthrough, assuming autobiographical tones. What does it mean to be Jewish? What did being Jewish mean for Derrida?

Excluded–included, outside–within, at the extreme margin, assailed by the 'identity disorder', Derrida could not help but bear witness to the impossibility of the self coinciding with the self. His Jewish identity was, certainly, not integral. Rather, it was incomplete, like the identity of any Jew. For Judaism puts into question the concept of 'identity' and points to the flaws in any identitarian thought. Already beforehand he had written: '*Juif* – Jew will be the other name for this impossibility of being self.'

Deconstruction alternates with narration. The landscape is the North-African coast, where in the past Spanish and Portuguese Jews have found asylum. When Derrida was born in El Biar in 1930, Algeria was a French colony; Arabs, Berbers, Sephardi Jews and 'Catholics' – as the French were called – lived there together. What dominated, for a Franco-Maghrebin Jew, was the neither–nor of extraneousness. All the more so, given that the Jewish community seemed hollowed out, having fallen prey to amnesia. The ever more sclerotic rituals, which had become external and illegible signs, were undercut by the ecclesiastical liturgy to the point of being transcribed into Christian language. 'The churches were being mimicked ... the "bar mitzvah" was called "communion" and

circumcision was named "baptism".'[11] This estrange-
ment and lack of culture were hardly helped by the
intimacy of a language like Yiddish, the protection and
resource of the Eastern Jews: the Algerian Sephardim
no longer spoke Judeo-Spanish, Ladino. The rupture
with France was consummated when the racial laws
were applied in 1940. Derrida lost French citizenship.
Expelled from the Ben Aknoun *lycée*, he continued his
education at the Alliance – the school hurriedly set up
by Jewish teachers, where he nonetheless felt out of
place, detached and distant, and developed an indelible
diffidence towards all community. It is to these circumstances that the trauma of the antisemitism inflicted by
the word *juif* [Jew] harks back. An unheard insult, an
affront coming from the outside, heavy with threat – 'a
wound, a denial of right rather than the right to belong
to a legitimate group', an 'original incrimination', a
blow, a projectile, which inserted itself into the body
marking out the letters J – U – I – F.

Fragments of memory, pained confessions, ironic
descriptions, are sprinkled across the texts, giving rise to
an autobiographical amnesia that deconstructs identity
through ambivalent formulas – paradoxical moves that
express gratitude and deny recognition. A Judaism *via*

11 Jacques Derrida, *Monolingualism of the Other; or, the
Prosthesis of Origin*, Stanford, CA, Stanford University Press,
1998, p. 54.

negationis gives way to a *judéité*, Jewishness, of a both broader and more ambitious meaning. Derrida shows his hand, regretting that he never learned the square letters: 'I neared the end without ever learning Hebrew.' There remained that void, that 'inner desert'. He reaffirms his 'non-belonging to Jewish culture', a peculiar way to attest to the exclusion within, though a relation nonetheless. He then finds a bold formula to express this: 'I am the last of the Jews.' What does 'last' mean? The most unworthy, the least faithful, the falsest, in short, the worst; but also the Jew after whom there may be no more Jews, who represents the death of Judaism, but also its chance of survival, because he bears the weight of the ultimate fidelity. A marrano, therefore.

'Ever more often, jokingly, but seriously, in recent years I have presented myself as a marrano.' Derrida wrote this in 2003. But already in *Circumfession* he had stated 'I am a sort of marrano of French Catholic culture.' Even here, this is not a full identification: 'une sorte de marrane' is limiting, allowing doubts and reservations to filter through. Yet it would be mistaken to believe that marrano is a metaphor or simulacrum. Derrida is here referring to history, to filiation, to his autobiographical research. There are countless traces of this. Starting with the name of his mother, Sultana Esther Georgette Safar Derrida, written on multiple occasions in different sequences and with some variations, including some allusions to 'St Esther'. If 'Jew' still sounded to Derrida as an insult hurled from the outside, 'marrano' instead awakened his loving affection: 'I have become enamoured with this word, which has become like an obsession.' Through its evocative power, its seductive force, it recalled the Judeo-Spanish world of his mother, that Andalusian splendour annihilated by the Inquisition. This is not a mania for genealogy, but rather the need for historical memory, fidelity to a secret that is passed down a feminine line, just as the most ancient marranism sought. And Derrida evokes the suggestive, ancient scene of the Friday evenings when – after all precautions had been taken and everything readied for potential interruption – his mother would light the Shabbat candles.

As in the case of the 'new Jews' of Amsterdam, for Derrida, too, marranism is specular – it has inevitable reflections. It exasperates and brings to light the non-coincidence of the Jew, who in the marrano reveals herself to be doubly extraneous, dissociated from the incomplete self, always in deconstruction. This gives some sense of why this autobiographical figure ended up becoming the secret cipher of his philosophy. Marranism is the only way to be Jewish. Thus Derrida admits: 'I am one of those marranos who do not call themselves Jews even in the secret of their heart, not so as to be authenticated as marranos on either side of the public frontier but because they doubt anything, they never confess, they never give up enlightenment, at whatever cost, ready to be burned.' What, then, remains of the marrano and of the Jew? There remains the fidelity to the secret that they have not chosen. 'It is for this reason that I call myself marrano: not out of the pilgrimages of a wandering Jew, not out of the series of exiles, but out of the clandestine search for a secret bigger and older than I am.'

The Secret of Remembrance – The Recollection of the Secret

In Jewish tradition, remembrance is an obligation – *zakhor*! The injunction is obsessively repeated throughout the Torah, giving life to the verses and underpinning the text. It is almost as if this were a desperate attempt to ward off the ineluctable drift towards forgetting. This act of recollection is fulfilled through the narration of the past. Thus, according to Yerushalmi, the Jewish people introduced the concept of 'history' – one destined to become a universal inheritance. The act of recollection is exercised through narration and rites. The great festivals become the commemoration of unrepeatable events like the exodus out of Egypt or the stay in the desert. And they are inserted in the weekly rhythm of the calendar in order to break it out of the natural cycle and mould it to history. Recollection is not contingent but is the hinge around which the community revolves.

It is then necessary to distinguish between memory and recollection, which are often confused. Memory is instinctive and unreflexive, left up to the spontaneity of the individual – it can thus fade away without a trace. Recollection, conversely, is entrusted to the community, which constitutes itself by observing it in the present. It recollects through observance and it is observant through recollection. The imperative *shamor!* [observe!] in fact comes next. It is directed at those who did not experience these events and are thus unable to have any memory of them. But they nonetheless have the responsibility of keeping recollection going, through observance. To practise recollection is to recall the past into the present with a view to the future. Narration, which maintains in words the recollection of the past event, discloses the possibility of commemoration, of taking part in memory, of participating in the community. To recount is already to redeem – and history is already a reparation.

Perhaps no one has grasped the distinction between memory and recollection better than Walter Benjamin. In place of the Hebrew *zekher*, in his German text there appears the word *Eingedenken* – thinking as one (*Ein*), remembering together with the defeated, in the conspiracy of a speech, which is now restored to them. The 'secret appointment' between the generations lies in this restitution. The liberating force of recollection does not impact the future alone, but also the past.

Already, simply because it relies on speech, which is something shared and brings people together, the act of recollection is not reducible to conserving the events of the past, frozen in the memory. Rather, it means rearticulating these events – for speech is rearticulated on each occasion. And thus it means bringing them into the present. This is indispensable, in a political reading that points, alarmed, to the emergency of the day. To read this past, which risks being erased and neglected, at the foundation of the present, is to redeem it by elevating it to a dignified standing in history.

Nonetheless, forgetting is not the only danger that threatens the past. Something else is also being transmitted – the 'winners' history'. This can prove even more 'catastrophic', because it cloaks the past in a cumulative memory, concealing it in the continuity of a reading that passes itself off as the truth and that seeks to impose itself as the mythology of the triumphant and erase any trace of the defeated. This is the bad-conscience memory, which aspires only to forget. Recollection must combat forgetting not only for the purpose of recollection – which would lead to its reification – but rather in the perspective of justice. That is why history is no irreversible process – the struggle is open and the outcome uncertain. But does the account of the defeated not itself risk succumbing to an apologetic temptation – in turn becoming a victorious epic? No, answers Benjamin. The history of the victims is radically other than that of the winners. It is not linear. Rather, it is marked by ruptures, faults, intermittences. It entertains a different relationship with the past and thus also with the future. For only the memory of the defeated is destined not to forget anything – neither the reign of the executioners of which it is the victim, nor the tradition of the victims, which it has the task of narrating. It assumes responsibility for that which remains illegible; it asks to be forever again retold, such that it does not sink into the abyss. It bears the weight of that which must not be forgotten.

But how could such recollection be perpetuated over the generations, if the rites were prohibited and there was a ban against the very texts that narrated the events that needed remembering? The forbidden memory disappeared and everything gradually slid into oblivion. Even the words appeared unreadable. Knowledge dimmed. It became impossible, then, to celebrate the festivals, which could no longer be called commemorations. Who could recite the entire Passover Haggadah – the account of the liberation out of Egypt? If the biblical narration could sometimes be useful, as far as the rest was concerned only small fragments could be saved from silence and darkness. Even the dates wavered; having been disguised, they ended up becoming uncertain. This was the difficulty the marranos bumped into.

The secret of recollection, which upheld and sustained Jewish history, was frustrated, as an unpractised work of recollection became hollowed out. Neither rites, nor words, nor gestures, nor obligations were handed down. There was almost nothing left to recollect, except the imperative of recollection itself. Moreover, the marrano betrayed the tradition in order to allow its survival, committed dishonesty in the name of truth, was unfaithful out of faithfulness. That is why recollection took on such extraordinary importance: it was the only remaining tie for those who had been segregated apart, the only bond with a tradition that would otherwise have met its end. The secret of recollection became the recollection of the secret.

In the night of clandestinity, in the absence of any historical witness, the marranos bore witness to the secret in an exasperated anachrony, a desperate resistance against the time of the dominant calendar. They fought on as they awaited a counter-history that would have been able to take over the reins from that secret. If they protected the secret through recollection, they would, perhaps, themselves be protected by the secret. But what does 'secret' mean? And how could one evoke it anew, or better, share it? The secret is inviolable, inaccessible, unwilling to come into the light, heterogeneous to speech, extraneous to appearance; it alludes to an irreversible resistance. Bathed in an esoteric aura, it however risked being mistaken, in a banal, if not malicious view, for an occult knowledge. It is as if the marranos were a secret society and not, instead, a community of the secret.

Or, perhaps, rather the secret does not have some remote meaning or content. It does not do so for the marrano – set apart from it and thus segregated, separated from it, she knows nothing of it. She must maintain the secret, out of respect for a unique relationship that subjects her to commitment and obligation; indeed doing so to the exclusion of all else. It is almost as if nothing remains of the ancient covenant except this bind. Only the demand of the secret still sanctions the pact, which, without that single response, that ultimate testimony, would finish forever. Thus the marranos are considered the last Jews, on the brink of an imminent epilogue. The final sparks of Judaism are the immense responsibility of each of them. That is why this secret, defended in the most intransigent silence, has survived any archive and cannot be stashed away therein.

Through the narrow alleyways of the old Jewish quarter of Palermo, in an inner courtyard of the *judería* of Toledo, next to the disturbing shadow of violence, there remains the recollection of an unviolated secret. Intimacy is the space reserved for the secret. But, just like the interior castle, this space is not a pristine fortress. Rather, it is riven by a crack, criss-crossed by an irreducible alterity. In the inner tribunal of the self, there lives a witness – extraneous and at the same time intimate – who separates and protects it. The self scrutinizes this within, where no one can extend their gaze. This is the space in which the ego constitutes itself, discovering the possibility of keeping a secret with the self. The marrano knows this and has tested it: for there to be a secret, the non-coincidence of the self with the self – duality, division – is indispensable. More than inhabit the crypt, the marrano is inhabited by it. The intimate space is excavated by the secret pact with the other. The marrano can then share this, because she is segregated from the secret, divided in her interiority.

Yet, complicit in their silence, the marranos share only the emptiness of the crypt. Something ineffable – the Name of God – brings them together. Hidden, exiled, dispersed, in a constellation of disaster, separated by a double extraneousness, they remain bound by the recollection of their secret, to which they no longer hold the key. Inaccessible and ultimately unknown, it is a secret of the secret. And this is something to which they do not hesitate to bear witness.

To Find Out More

Despite the difficulty of finding documentary sources, there is no lack of historical reconstructions regarding the marranos. The work in the archives has not, however, been followed by in-depth philosophical, political and theological reflection. As well as the two-volume work by Yitzhak Baer, *Die Juden im christlichen Spanien. Urkunden und Regesten*, 2 volumes, Akademie für die Wissenschaft des Judentums, Berlin, 1929–36 – a classic, albeit one with many limits – there is also Cecil Roth, *A History of the Marranos*, Varda Books, Skokie, IL, 2001 [1932]. The collection of lectures given by Fritz Heymann, *Morte o battesimo. Una storia di marrani*, edited by J. H. Schoeps, Giuntina, Florence, 2007, should, for its part, be taken as a piece of testimony. Another classic is Américo Castro, *La realidad histórica de España*, Porrua, Mexico City, 1955. Dated, but also significant, are the contributions by Israël Salvato Révah, now collected in

Des marranes à Spinoza, edited by H. Méchoulan, P.-F. Moreau and C. L. Wilke, Vrin, Paris, 1995. Of further importance are the works of Yosef Hayim Yerushalmi, largely gathered in *Sefardica. Essais sur l'histoire des Juifs, des marranes & des nouveaux-chrétiens d'origine hispano-portugaise*, preface by Y. Kaplan, Chandeigne, Paris, 2016. Worth mentioning by this same author is *From Spanish Court to Italian Ghetto: Isaac Cardoso: A Study in Seventeenth-Century Marranism and Jewish Apologetics*, University of Washington Press, Seattle, 1981. Leon Poliakov dedicated part of his research to the marranos, in *The History of Anti-Semitism: From Mohammed to Marranos*, Vanguard Press, New York, 1973. On the marranos' religion, one fundamental work is David M. Gitlitz, *Secrecy and Deceit. The Religion of the Crypto-Jews*, University of New Mexico Press, Albuquerque, 2002. A further point of reference is Nathan Wachtel, *The Faith of Remembrance: Marrano Labyrinths,* University of Pennsylvania Press, Philadelphia, 2013, as well as his *Entre Moïse et Jésus. Études marranes (XV–XXI siècle)*, CNRS Éditions, Paris, 2013.

An interest in the 'returning' marranos has emerged ever more frequently in recent years. Other than Wachtel's studies regarding Brazil, this return by North American crypto-Jews is reconstructed by Janet Liebman Jacobs, *Hidden Heritage. The Legacy of the Crypto-Jews*, University of California Press, Berkeley, 2002. However, there is no comprehensive research concerning present-day (rather than past) marranism in Italy, especially in the South, where this phenomenon continues to display matchless energy. The rediscovery of contemporary marranisms is also the theme of the miscellany edited by Jacques Ehrenfreund and Jean-Philippe Schreiber, *Les marranismes. De la religiosité cachée à la société ouverte*, Demopolis, Paris, 2014.

In cultural history, José Faur authored a pioneering study, *In the Shadow of History. Jews and Conversos at the Dawn of Modernity*, State University of New York Press, Albany, 1992. Yirmiyahu Yovel continued in this same vein with *The Other Within. The Marranos. Split Identity and Emerging Modernity*, Princeton University Press, Princeton/Oxford, 2009. Gianluca Solla, *Marrani: Il debito segreto*, Marietti, Genoa/Milan, 2008, represents a reflection all of its own. On diaspora and its effects, see Jonathan and Daniel Boyarin, *Powers of Diaspora: Two Essays on the Relevance of Jewish Culture*, University of Minnesota, Minneapolis, 2002. It is also worth citing the volume edited by Shmuel Trigano, *Le Juif caché: Marranisme et modernité*, Pardès, Grez-sur-Loing, 2000.

One highly controversial question concerns whether, as some historians claim, the phenomenon of marranism ought to be archived forever, or if one ought instead to speak of a marrano condition that transcends the limits of any historical definition – especially when faced with the re-emergence of this phenomenon. One who does archive the question is the historian Claude B.

Stuczynski, who wrote, among other things, the entry on *Marranesimo* in the *Dizionario storico dell'Inquisizione*, edited by A. Prosperi, Scuola Normale Superiore, Pisa, 2010, vol. 3, pp. 989–96. At the other end of the spectrum are, for example, Jacques Revel, 'Une condition marrane?', in *Annales HSS*, 2002, pp. 335–45, and Jacques Derrida. His thoughts on this theme are rather scattered across several essays, but one can also read his quasi-autobiographical reflection in Geoffrey Bennington and Jacques Derrida, *Jacques Derrida*, University of Chicago Press, Chicago, 1999. On this theme, see the recent *The Marrano Specter: Derrida and Hispanism,* edited by E. G. Ziffin, foreword by Peggy Kamuf, afterword by Geoffrey Bennington, Fordham University Press, New York, 2017. Risky, however, is the tendency to make the marrano into a metaphor, as happens here and there in some essays, especially works of comparative literature.

There are numerous recent specialist historical studies. For example, the miscellany edited by Pier Cesare Ioly Zorattini, *L'identità dissimulata. Giudaizzanti iberici nell'Europa cristiana dell'età moderna*, Olschki, Florence, 2002; Miriam Bodian, *Hebrews of the Portuguese Nation. Conversos and Community in Early Modern Amsterdam*, Indiana University Press, Bloomington, 2000; and Natalia Muchnik, *De paroles et de gestes. Constructions marranes en terre d'Inquisition*, EHESS, Paris, 2014.

It would, however, be impossible to provide even a rough panorama of the studies dedicated to the thinkers of Amsterdam, or indeed of the essays on the marrano provenance of writers, philosophers and intellectuals from Cervantes to Pessoa and from Montaigne to Proust.